Special Technology
for Special Children

Special Technology for Special Children

Computers to Serve
Communication and Autonomy in the
Education of Handicapped Children

by E. Paul Goldenberg, Ed.D.
Bolt Beranek and Newman, Inc.
Cambridge, Massachusetts

University Park Press
Baltimore

UNIVERSITY PARK PRESS
International Publishers in Science, Medicine, and Education
233 East Redwood Street
Baltimore, Maryland 21202

Composed by University Park Press, Typesetting Division
Manufactured in the United States of America by The Maple Press Company

Library of Congress Cataloging in Publication Data
Goldenberg, Ernest Paul.
   Special technology for special children.
   Bibliography: p.
   Includes index.
   1.   Handicapped children — Education. 2.   Computer-assisted instruction. I.   Title. [DNLM: 1.   Handicap-ped. 2.   Education, Special. 3.   Computer assisted instruction. LC4015 G618s]
LC4019.G64   371.9'043   79-11565
ISBN 0-8391-1441-9

Contents

Figures vii
Preface ix
Acknowledgments. xi

Part I   Special Education

Chapter 1   The Handicap as Sociological and Technological
   Artifact   3
   The Book   4
   The History   5
   The Philosophy   9
   The Psychology   12
   The Economics   13
   The Experiments   15
Chapter 2   Normal Needs and Special Needs   19
   Normal Needs   20
   The Computer Meeting Normal Needs — Two Metaphors   21
   Special Needs   23
   Three Ways Computers Can Be Used in Education   25
   Information, Self-Expression, and Feedback   28
   Where to Focus: Behavior or Experience   30

Part II   Special Children

Chapter 3   Cerebral Palsy, Motor Experience, and Cognitive
   Development   35
   The Children   36
   The Theorists — Cognitive Development Depends on
      Activity   39
   Cognition without Activity — A Puzzle   42
   Some Conjectured Solutions to the Dilemma.   49
   A Brief Restatement   50
Chapter 4   Deafness, Language, and Cognitive Development   53
   The Children   54
   The Educational Handicap of Deafness   58
   Issues in Deaf Education   60
   The Salvos in the Hundred-Years' War.   61
   Language and Thinking   64

Chapter 5 **Autism, Perception, and Cognitive Development** 71
    Cognitively Handicapped Children 72
    The Characteristics of Autism 82
    Autistic Children in School 88
    The Symptom as a Healthy, Adaptive Effort 89

Part III Special Technology

Chapter 6 **Communicating with the Computer** 95
    Drawing with the Turtle 96
    Input Schemes 101
    Tailoring Communication to the Child 105
Chapter 7 **Novel Sources of Control, Activity, and Meaning** 117
    Novel Sources of Control for the Physically Handi-
        capped Child 119
    Novel Sources of Activity for the Deaf Child 126
    Novel Sources of Meaning for the Autistic Child 140

Part IV Research Needs

Chapter 8 **Research Needs** 149
    Explorations 150
    Research and Development for Service Delivery 152
    Basic Research 153
    Clinical Definitions 156
    New Colleagues 157
    Teaching toward Strengths 157
    Demographic Studies 157
    Setting Priorities 158
Appendix: Two Videotape Transcriptions
    Peter 161
    Philip 164

    References 169
    Index 177

Figures

Figure 1. Jane with robot turtle 14
Figure 2. A makeshift command-scanner 37
Figure 3. The slot machine with some cards in it 73
Figure 4. The aim-the-arrow game 77
Figure 5. The drawing screen and command scanner 97
Figure 6. Turning the turtle left 120° 98
Figure 7. Saving a drawing 98
Figure 8. Two sides and two turns completed 99
Figure 9. Three sides and three turns completed 99
Figure 10. The square 100
Figure 11. Starting the turtle facing "west" 100
Figure 12. Square with turtle at the top 101
Figure 13. House with a bug 102
Figure 14. Square with turtle prepared to make a roof 102
Figure 15. The house 103
Figure 16. Selecting the row of numbers 104
Figure 17. Selecting the number 5 105
Figure 18. TO MOM 110
Figure 19. FORWARD 80 RC 90 111
Figure 20. FORWARD 80 LC 90 111
Figure 21. FORWARD 80 RIGHT 90 LC 90 112
Figure 22. TO GOING 112
Figure 23. TO DADS 113
Figure 24. TO JAY 113
Figure 25. Laurie's design 114
Figure 26. Jonny's first drawing of a wheelchair 114
Figure 27. Electronic data tablet 123
Figure 28. Approaching the terminal 141
Figure 29. Making a choice on a touch-sensitive screen 142

Preface

Writing an interdisciplinary book for psychologists, educators, rehabilitation professionals, and scientists in the field of artificial intelligence has unique rewards, but it also has special difficulties.

The rewards come from the prospect of helping these various specialists come together to share their insights with professionals from other intellectual worlds. Building a house requires people with different skills to work together. Moving toward solutions to the multifaceted problems of the handicapped is certainly no less complicated.

The difficulties in writing this book have been primarily ones of communication. I have tried to explain specialized concepts when they first appear so that terminology will not stand in the way of this needed interchange. I have also labored (with considerable help from my friends) to provide this background in a way that would not bog the reader down in a morass of preliminaries and, ultimately, no story.

This book is organized in four parts. In the first part, Chapters 1 and 2 present a philosophy of educating handicapped children and the role that computers can play in that process. Chapter 1 gives a brief historical perspective and describes the scope of the experiments that led to the preparation of this book. Chapter 2 focuses on alternative philosophies of education and explains the rationale for the philosophy that fostered these experiments.

Chapters 3, 4, and 5 of Part II focus on the handicaps themselves, providing the reader with selected issues in the psychology and education of three groups of handicapped children, physically handicapped, deaf, and autistic children, respectively. The issues that I feel are ultimately most germane to the development of computer-based educational environments and aids are discussed in the light of recent research and professional opinion. Each chapter begins with brief case studies of the children whose work with computers inspired this book.

In Part III, Chapters 6 and 7 are concerned with the computer technology. Chapter 6 describes the computer hardware and software used in my experiments. Chapter 7 elaborates on the technologies that, although well developed themselves, have not yet been made to work *together* in service of the handicapped. Chapter 7 also makes specific suggestions for the use of that technology.

The final part, Chapter 8, is devoted to summarizing the research issues that I encountered in the process of writing this book. Not all of these issues were raised by my experiments — some were encountered as I tried, myself, to do the background research to explain my own findings.

It is my fervent hope that the professional who knows computers well, but has never tried teaching a handicapped child, as well as the therapist who has never used a computer, will find this book readable and will be encouraged to develop joint projects with professionals he or she had never thought of working with before.

Acknowledgments

This book grew out of a very exciting investigation that began while I worked with the Logo Group in the Artificial Intelligence Laboratory of Massachusetts Institute of Technology. To cite separately all of the individuals who participated in the realization of this work would involve listing most of the members of the Logo Group and of the Crotched Mountain Center, Greenfield, New Hampshire, where part of the work was done. Other important influences came from mentors and colleagues at Bolt Beranek and Newman, Inc., Cambridge, Massachusetts and at the Harvard Graduate School of Education.

I am genuinely eager to mention a small few whose contributions were particularly great.

From MIT

— Bruce Edwards, a computer scientist in artificial intelligence research at the Artificial Intelligence Laboratory at MIT, was on 24-hour emergency call for hardware and software modifications that were needed to adapt the Logo Group's computers to this special use. He also assisted us at Crotched Mountain in documenting this work.

— Ellen Hildreth, currently conducting artificial intelligence research in vision at MIT, was centrally involved with the project from its very inception. Her contributions to all phases of planning, teaching, documentation, and evaluation were absolutely vital and thoroughly appreciated.

— Margaret Minsky, currently on the staff of the Logo Group, helped with the teaching both in the laboratory and at Crotched Mountain.

— Seymour Papert, director of the Logo Group, participated in the design of the project and in the actual teaching.

The EMG work (described in Chapter 7) was pioneered by a very exciting group of high school students who were in my "handicapped" section of a National Science Foundation summer science session directed by Hal Abelson and Andy diSessa at the Logo Group. Two other high school students, Henry Minsky and Jon Miller, did considerable work in programming and modifying the programs for use by the visiting handicapped children. To all of these people, many of whom are now studying biomedical applications of technology in college, my sincere thanks.

From the Crotched Mountain Center

— Clinton Hilliard, speech pathologist and former director of the Communication Department at the Mountain (now head of Speech Pathology at Hawthorne

Children's Center, Hawthorne, Mass.), worked behind the scenes to support this project and was instructive, inspirational, and warm to all the project staff.

— Dan Steinberg, former director of Physical and Occupational Therapy at the Mountain who has since left and whose loss we felt sharply, kept bringing the Mountain to MIT until MIT was convinced to go to the Mountain.

Special mention should be made of Leo Geoffrion of the University of New Hampshire, and The Communication and Learning Group, Inc. (CLG), Durham, N.H. who initially introduced me to Dan Steinberg and who, with Dan, first shifted my attention to cerebral palsied children. Leo has also made valuable intellectual and editorial contributions to the numberless early drafts of this book when it was still a long paper, and he has generously offered me data from his CARIS project, some of which is reported for the first time in this book.

I feel acutely aware of the impossibility of crediting all the sources of ideas that have crept into this work, but feel it important to mention the influence that the many conversations with Hermine Sinclair (then at MIT), Harold Abelson (MIT), Richard Rubinstein (BBN), William Perry, and Courtney Cazden (both of Harvard) have had on my thinking when this document was first being prepared. Thinking out the contents of Chapter 7 took place with the help of many valuable discussions with Wally Feurzeig, Mario Grignetti, Bill Huggins, and Vince Manis (all of BBN), and Margaret Press at the Boston College Campus School. Later, particularly as this work began evolving into a book, others came to influence it strongly, particularly Ursula and John Willis and my wife, Cindy Carter, all of CLG. Besides supplying moral support, which was frequently in short supply during the final intensive grind, Cindy has made numerous contributions to the organization and editing of this book. Principally in the summary to Chapter 4, but throughout the book as well, she has added importantly to the ideas and the writing.

Offering help to read through rough drafts, even under short deadlines, and to make suggestions has to be an act of great courage! Roy Carter and Roz Kaplan volunteered for that task anyway. It was help that I genuinely appreciated.

Finally, I had never before understood the significance of acknowledging the patient and long-suffering friends and relatives of the writer. Now I do. With a lot of love, thank you!

This book is lovingly dedicated to Jane, whose bright eyes convinced me there was a lot of work to do, whose smile convinced me to do the work, and whose movements inspired many of the ideas I have described

To Bruce and JJ who, with Jane, allowed me to use their photographs and names to beautify this book

To the children I've called Susan and Ricky, Phillip, Peter and Gordon, Nancy, Joey, Kevin, Thomas and Annette, Joshua and Gary, Jay, Johnny, Laurie and Cheryl, Jan and Anna

To the dozens of other children not mentioned in this book who directly helped in the project and to their classmates and to those who love them

In the hopes that we all may learn to know these children better and become better teachers and friends for them.

Special Technology
for Special Children

Part I
Special Education

Chapter 1
The Handicap as Sociological and Technological Artifact

THE BOOK

Throughout this book, I refer to deaf children, cerebral palsied children, and autistic children, sometimes almost in the same breath. I have no intention of suggesting that these children's life problems are all the same, nor do I believe that the solutions are all the same. However, it is not their "special" needs with which I am primarily concerned, but their "normal" needs. What binds these children together also binds them to the rest of humanity: their needs to have an enjoyable and estimable life and to be able to interact satisfyingly with their environment and its people, things, and demands. Sometimes we require special techniques and technology to help us meet our needs. Only when these are wanting are we truly handicapped.

One old and readily available technology is eyeglasses, without which multitudes of bright people would be virtually ineducable and severely disabled in a society such as ours. This book examines an emerging technology that holds promise of eradicating some of the handicaps inherent in cerebral palsy, deafness, and autism.

Over the past decade, exciting projects have been undertaken in which young children are given the opportunity to "play" with computers that are specially designed to be the children's servants. Children can use the computer to draw pictures, to create and solve puzzles, to compose stories, and to play games. The nearly universal observation has been that these children are highly enthusiastic about the computer. Most of these average children rapidly develop sufficient mastery of the computer to enable them to demonstrate ability far beyond that seen or even deemed possible in their regular schoolwork. The special child's interaction with the world is limited in more ways than the normal child's. It is limited once, "naturally," by his handicap, and again, artificially, by us in our misunderstandings of the handicap. It is therefore an even more strikingly significant event in that child's life to become the master of a powerful technology. It was this realization that motivated my work with the handicapped.

Of course, one cannot talk intelligently about the virtues of a technology without considering the context in which it is found and the use to which it is put. For this reason, I bring the light of research in linguistics, neurology, education, and psychology into my discussion of our

The term *sociological and technological artifact* was expressed by John B. Eulenberg (1976) in his presentation at the Conference on Systems and Devices for the Disabled.

understandings (and misunderstandings) of children with a variety of handicaps.

A principal theme throughout this book is that the computer provides a flexible technology that can so thoroughly enrich the experiences and communication of certain handicapped persons that activities and learning that were previously thought impossible for them become routine and easy. By facilitating communication and activity for these persons, this technology provides a window into their minds that radically changes the picture we, and they, have of their abilities.

The tremendous potential for revolutionizing evaluation and education for the handicapped has already been realized on a tiny scale in brief preliminary studies. Impacts extend to the economics and sociology of handicaps as well as to developmental and cognitive psychology. Most important is the realistic promise that dignity and fulfillment can be infused into lives that are now crushed and wasted. My ultimate intention is to present a picture of a social and technological environment within which such vast improvements in the quality of life of a handicapped individual can be realized that we, and, importantly, the individual, can begin seeing his life, like that of the person with eyeglasses, as normal.

The deaf child's difficulties originate as input problems. The cerebral palsied child's difficulties originate as output problems. The autistic child has multiple processing problems whose origins are, as yet, unclear. That the computer can be useful over this wide range of problems indicates its flexibility. In each case, the computer meets the child's need for an appropriate modality through which the child is able to interact and communicate freely with his environment.

THE HISTORY

The application of electronic technology to aid communication for the severely handicapped person is not, relative to the technology itself, a new idea. Electrical communication aids for the physically handicapped have been reported as far back as 1957 (LaVoy, 1957) and continue to appear sporadically in the literature.[1]

Despite the availability, variety, and power of these devices — and despite the age of some of them — they are not yet well known or widely

[1]The best current references citing a wide variety of these devices are Vanderheiden and Grilley (1976) and Vanderheiden (1978). Other current researchers of note include Kafafian (1973), Foulds and Gaddis (1975), Rosen and Durfee (1978), and Rowell, Dalrymple, and Olsen (1978).

used. One recent text on cerebral palsied children (Marks, 1974) makes no mention of electronic adaptive equipment, biofeedback, or computers, despite the presence of an entire chapter devoted to adaptive devices. A more recent and comprehensive volume on cerebral palsy (Cruickshank, 1976) devotes a chapter to "the development of communication skills" (Lencione, 1976) that contains a few pages on mechanical language boards and other aids for aphonic communication but gives no indication of the prevalence or success of their use in the field.

It is disappointing, but not surprising, to note that little word of existing applications of technology has filtered into the standard texts. The existence of a true field devoted to electronic aids for the handicapped is so new that communication, even among the concerned professionals, still tends to be sluggish and spotty. However, in some areas of the field communication is improving. "An international organization of hobbyists interested in handicapped applications," named Computers for the Handicapped, was formed in 1977 (Suding, 1978). The Spring of 1978 saw the publication of a quarterly newsletter, *Communication Outlook,* that was the first official communication vehicle devoted to "the needs of the growing community of individuals throughout the world who are concerned with technological aids to communication" (Eulenberg and Vanderheiden, 1978). Unfortunately, various conferences on the subject still tend not to represent either the breadth or the depth of work that actually exists. Reference to three very recent conferences may help to illustrate this.

On October 18, 1977, the Congressional Subcommittee on Domestic and International Scientific Planning, Analysis, and Cooperation and the Subcommittee on Select Education, chaired by Congressman Scheuer, held hearings specifically concerned with computers and the handicapped. These subcommittees compiled a list of expert witnesses (representatives from industry and research) who could demonstrate the advances that have been made in computer technology for the handicapped.

The conference topic ostensibly included all the handicapped, and yet the devices that were shown dealt exclusively with the blind and motorically handicapped. Except for one very brief mention of the deaf, no other handicapped group was mentioned at all.

These omissions are striking. The deaf population is quite large — there are 6.5 million deaf persons in the United States alone; a half million of these deaf persons are under age 19, and about half of these young persons were deaf before they learned language (Schein and Delk, 1974). The social and intellectual isolation caused by this devastating handicap must not be discounted.

The number of people with cognitive handicaps, perceptual handicaps or learning disabilities is even greater than the number of deaf persons. The diagnosis of mental retardation, alone, is made for more than 6 million Americans — about 3% of the population — according to the most generally accepted prevalence rate. U.S. Senate Report 93-1169 indicates that a half million school-age children have specific learning disabilities and some 80,000 children are severely handicapped by autism. Despite these numbers, neither the invited witnesses nor the subcommittees made any mention whatsoever of the needs of these people or of the potential for computers to help meet their needs.

The same bias is seen in professional meetings as well. Consider, for example, the 5th Annual Conference on Systems and Devices for the Disabled, held in June, 1978, in Houston, Texas. Despite the explicit inclusion of deafness in their call for papers dealing with all handicaps, only 2 out of the 60 presentations touched that topic. Only one of these (Rubinstein and Goldenberg, 1978) described a computer application. Again, no mention whatsoever was made of any technology for the cognitively or perceptually impaired or learning disabled person. The same orientation could be seen in the 1978 proceedings of the West Coast Computer Faire and, for that matter, in literature searches through the ERIC and Exceptional Child data bases. Even article titles, themselves, are prone to this bias. "Microcomputer-based Sensory Aids for the Handicapped" (Brugler, 1978) describes five devices, three of which are aids exclusively for the blind, one of which is described in terms of its usefulness for the blind but is potentially useful for the nonvocal, and the last of which is a screening device intended not to aid a handicapped person, but to detect one.

To have a full appreciation of the status of computers for the handicapped, not only must we recognize that large areas seem underrepresented, but also we must put some of the existing reports of technological advances into perspective. Nye (1972), referring to aids for the visually impaired, comments that the complexity of some of the tasks for which these devices are designed is

> too often. . . overlooked or underestimated and many devices (some of which are conceived over and over again) made demands on the skills of the user which go well beyond his ability to respond. Thus he is unable to operate the device at the speeds which are required in practical situations. For example, he may be able to read by ear or touch using a simple acoustic or tactile transducer but so slowly that boredom rapidly sets in and the device is soon rejected except for very limited tasks.

Nye's comments, although made in 1972, are not outdated. Equally strong comments might be made concerning communication aids for mo-

torically handicapped individuals. Several such devices were reported at
the 5th Annual Conference on Systems and Devices for the Disabled. One
device that was described certainly seemed to make heavy demands on the
user:

> Letters, numbers or symbols are selected by the user from a list displayed on
> the CRT.... The lists from which the user selects characters [are ten charac-
> ters long]. Only one list is displayed at a time. When a list is initially dis-
> played, the cursor is positioned over the first character. Puffing [into a tube
> containing a pressure sensitive switch] advances the cursor one character at a
> time along the list, resetting to the beginning when the end of the list is
> reached. A sip input when the cursor is positioned over a character causes
> that character or the action associated with it to be selected. (Doubler, Chil-
> dress, and Strysik, 1978)

Given available technologies, the selection of letters described above
seems ludicrously slow and cumbersome. It is hard not to picture an already handicapped person gasping and panting after an involved message. However, we must not be so critical of the shortcomings of this device that we overlook its important contributions. Its developers included
in their design a truly excellent feature, a message editing capability. Few
of us think or type flawlessly, so editing a message is very important, especially when the initial effort required to create the message is very great.

A final requirement, if we are to understand how computers can help
handicapped persons, is that we must understand the handicaps as well. It
is important to separate folk wisdom from fact in many areas. If this is to
happen, specialists from several fields, such as engineers, educators,
physicians, and psychologists, and the intended users themselves, must
share their collective knowledge and experience in designing any device.
For example, if we wish to create a better reading aid for the blind, it is important to realize that, of all the people whose sight is so poor that they
cannot use their vision for reading, only about 3% of them use Braille.
We must not mistakenly assume that the problems of the blind would be
solved merely by a new and better Braille transcription device.

Similar remarks must be made about the communication devices for
nonvocal physically disabled persons. Making communication possible
for these persons is a tremendous achievement. However, making it fluent
and practical is yet to be achieved, and unfortunately this point was not
emphasized at the Congressional hearings.

Until recently, even though the power of microelectronics is increas-
ing and costs of hardware are plummeting, communicators for the handicapped have remained inflexible. Communicators did what they were designed to do, but they could not grow with the user as his skills expanded,

or they grew, but only a little and only at the initiative of a caregiver. Even now that microelectronics has flooded the rehabilitation research field, there remains a strong tendency to underuse its power and to build devices that cannot be modified and upgraded by their users.

The surface has barely been scratched in the educational/therapeutic uses of computers for handicapped children. Colby (1973, 1975) and Weir and Emanuel (1976) used the computer to catalyze communication in an autistic child. Despite the fact that much of Colby's rationale was published in 1971 (Colby and Smith, 1971) this field remains essentially unexplored today. Two more projects of this sort recently have been begun (Geoffrion and Bergeron, 1978; O'Brien, 1977), but the results are not yet available.

Computer technologies to aid in speech training have been designed for use with deaf persons (Nickerson and Stevens, 1973; Boothroyd et al., 1975; Nickerson, Kalikow, and Stevens, 1976). Some workers have concentrated on academic drill and practice (Suppes, 1971; Fletcher and Beard, 1973), sometimes using attractive, game-like activities (Dugdale and Vogel, 1978). Layzer (1976) has described a system that "textures" the presentation of written English for the deaf, presenting a visual analogue of the rhythmical and metrical properties of spoken poetry or song.

Job training in computer careers has been designed for deaf or physically handicapped adults, but these training programs assume that the person is already ready for job training, if not, in fact, ready for the job (Yasaki, 1975; *COBOL Instruction for Handicapped,* 1976).

THE PHILOSOPHY

Cultural lag is certainly part of the reason that communication aids are neither in wide use nor, for the most part, in good use where they are known. But more is involved than merely the time it takes to sell the world on a new product. It is my contention that the central problem is that our technological knowhow and philosophical outlooks are out of phase with each other.

What we try to accomplish — and, perhaps more to the point, what we do not try to accomplish — in habilitation and education of the handicapped is limited by what tools and techniques we have available and by what ultimate success we expect is possible. It is also influenced by our view, perhaps limited by our "normal" ethnocentrism, of what a normal life must include (Vernon and Makowsky, 1969). Thus, we may strive for goals that are unrealistic and basically unnecessary, thereby frustrating the handicapped person. At the same time, we may reject goals that seem to us unattainable, but that could be expected with a more appropriate pedagogy or technology. Consider, for example, a study that showed the effectiveness of music in improving the life of the long-term institutionalized mental patient. The study called for installation of a stereo system on a ward and then for the measurement of the rate of the patients' daytime pants-wetting, which was shown to decrease. I have no doubt that the patients did, indeed, wet their pants less frequently, nor do I question the validity of that observation as a measure of the improvements of their lives — not to mention the lives of their attendants. Certainly, one cannot question the importance of improving the lives of these people in any way, no matter how small. However, one should contrast that research on improved living with the unfortunately less common view of Alan J. White, director of Project SEARCH, in Programs for the Handicapped:

> [Connecticut] has long had good programs to develop high creative potential among schoolchildren where it was found to exist, but only in the last year has a serious effort been made to look for these talents among children who have learning disabilities or emotional disturbances, or who are so crippled or palsied they cannot work or talk or hold a pencil to paper.
> By extensive and innovative testing, it was found that 12 percent of the handicapped children who were studied were gifted, roughly three times as many as in the general school population. . . .
> The first surprise. . . was that two-thirds of the handicapped children. . . were capable of being tested. They had expected to be able to test a quarter of them at most. "This group has exceptional potential for growth and training and creative activity in the arts," Mr. White said. He suspected that families and teachers looked too seldom for the creative spark that might be there, because they spent all their agony and attention on the child's handicap. "They look for the defects and try to bring these up to strength," Mr. White said. "When a child does have a strength, the parents turn away from it and say, 'Thank goodness we don't have to do anything about that.' My feeling is we should be building on those strengths." (U.S. Department of Health, Education and Welfare, 1976)

If Mozart had had a severe speech defect that was given more attention than his piano playing, we would never have heard of him! Consider how our perception of the mildly myopic person is affected by our knowledge of how to make and use eyeglasses. How vast a segment of our population would be ineducable and unemployable without this technology and would, no doubt, seem intellectually and socially retarded in our current and complex society!

A handicap is a sociological artifact to the extent that we see a person with glasses as normal, but a person with a hearing aid as handicapped. In our efforts to pursue the normal routes to education and growth, we may overlook aids that are already available. An electric toothbrush may be a luxury for a normal person, but for Jane (described in Chapter 2), who cannot open her mouth much and cannot hold it open reliably, it is an essential tool for dental hygiene. Yet no child on Jane's ward owns one and no hospital or governmental regulation seems to mandate such purchases. The technology exists, but it is not being used.

Furthermore, those adaptations that make life more convenient for a handicapped individual are often not as readily accepted as aids for normal persons. Even the beneficiaries sometimes come to regard special adaptations as second best.[2] The cosmetics of an aid for normal people — let us say a remote control switch for the TV — would never be ignored by the manufacturer, but similar consideration for the attractiveness of a device and the dignity of its user is not so universal in the design of aids for people identified as handicapped. A speech pathologist tells of his experience with two kinds of wheelchairs. When he travels about in his standard wheelchair and children look at him, their mothers would say "Don't look at that man; he's sick." When he travels on his bright yellow, sleek, electric motorized "golf-cart" wheelchair and children look at him, their mothers even encourage the curiosity (personal communication from Hilliard, while he was director of Communication Therapy at Crotched Mountain Center, Greenfield, New Hampshire).

The handicap is a technological artifact as well. We are quite skilled at making aids to correct severely defective vision. Glasses are small, inex-

---

[2]An interesting case in point is sign language (Markowicz, 1972; Woodward, 1973). A casual look at the society of deaf adults tells us that signing is not merely an interim way for the child to communicate, and yet, for the most part, even the schools that most freely accept signed communication tend to regard the language ethnocentrically, treating it only as an auxiliary language, something which may be valued as a kind of teaching tool, but never esteemed as much as English. David M. Denton, Superintendent of the Maryland School for the Deaf, must certainly be considered a strong and conscientious supporter of total communication for deaf children. In an article supporting its use (Denton, 1970), he quotes the definition of total communication: "By total communication is meant the RIGHT of a deaf child to learn to use all forms of communication available to develop *language competence*. This includes the full spectrum, child devised gestures, speech, formal signs, fingerspelling, speechreading, reading and writing" (p. 5, italics mine). Perhaps no special emphasis was intended when "language competence" was chosen instead of something like "intellectual strength, the knowledge of self-worth and social fluency," but neither have I seen explicit acknowledgment that language is not an end, but a means. Is American Sign Language ever taught to deaf children with the same deliberate care and pride that characterizes the teaching of English to either hearing or deaf children?

pensive, unobtrusive, attractive, portable, and effective. Many people who wear glasses would be "lost without them" and utterly barred from the educational, vocational, and recreational lives they now lead. We are not as skilled at making aids to correct even moderately defective hearing. There are hearing-impaired individuals who are able to use an amplified telephone perfectly well without their hearing aids, but who cannot, even with the aids, understand relatively loud speech in daily person-to-person conversations without depending on speechreading, gesture, or heavy contextual cues. Although the technology is now available, existing communication aids for the severely physically handicapped are at an even more primitive level than hearing aids; true communication requires much more than slow text production.

THE PSYCHOLOGY

The experiments described in this text are a source of new and valuable data about developmental processes. Much of current cognitive psychological theory is dominated by the idea that passive observation of our environment is insufficient for learning, whether that learning is at the perceptual organizational level or whether it involves the so-called higher cognitive processes. Serious problems are posed for this kind of theory, when a severely physically handicapped person who has never passed normally through the sensorimotor stage of development is able, after a few minutes of computer training, to match in style and detail the typical performance of a bright, able-bodied fifth grader on a drawing task that requires considerable sensitivity to the perception of angle and dimension. Such has been our experience with a cerebral palsied adolescent, Jay, who has never had speech or any use of his arms or legs. (Jay's work is described in greater detail in Chapter 6.)

Moreover, such fast and dramatic effects have by no means been limited to a few of the children with whom I worked. Having access to a powerful technology in which one can control oneself and with which one can experiment and get direct, immediate feedback creates such a striking change in these children's sense of autonomy that it is not surprising that they typically perform "miracles" in their first few minutes working with the computer. For example, an autistic adolescent (see "Joey" in Chapter 5), observed to be mute and assumed to be deaf, spoke his first words to a robot turtle. Child after child assumed to be mentally retarded showed clear evidence of normal or better intellectual ability (e.g., "Susan" in Chapter 3). These "surprises" give important lessons in the handling of the severely handicapped individual and raise hard questions about currently accepted theories as well as clinical practice.

THE ECONOMICS

It is estimated that nearly 100,000 physically disabled individuals with adequate sensory, perceptual, and cognitive capabilities for language are unable to communicate vocally as a result of their condition, and nearly 300,000 individuals are unable to write.[3] The technology required to ameliorate this communication handicap currently exists, at least at the prototype level. None of it depends on designs or devices that could not be available within a matter of months. The human payoffs are, therefore, quite realistic.

Furthermore, the alternative for most of these physically disabled persons is a life of total support from governmental and private agencies. The cost of such support during the school-age years is frequently as high as $20,000 per year and is rising rapidly. For adults the costs may be slightly lower, but services are drastically limited. Estimates of lifetime support for an institutionalized, totally disabled person range upward from $500,000.

No matter how much we improve the educational and recreational aspects of the handicapped person's life, we are still only providing Band-Aids until we can solve the enormously tragic feeling of uselessness. A life spent vegetating expensively, even with stereo, just cannot compare with a self-supporting life of personally meaningful and satisfying activity. Jobs exist that depend more on the manipulation of information than on the manipulation of things. Jobs, therefore, in principle, are accessible via the computer even to the most severely physically handicapped persons.

---

[3]These figures are based on estimates derived at the Bureau of Education for Handicapped Conference on Communication Aids for the Severely Physically Handicapped. Government participants in the group that derived these estimates included Allan Dittmann of Bureau of Education of the Handicapped, Lyle Lloyd of the National Institute of Child Health and Human Development, and Christie Ludlow of the National Institute of Neurological and Communicative Diseases and Stroke. Non-government participants included Kenneth M. Colby, Terry DeBriere, John B. Eulenberg, Richard Foulds, Haig Kafafian, Maurice LeBlanc, Gregg C. Vanderheiden, and myself. A distinction was made between "nonverbal," "nonvocal" and "nonwriting" persons. The first group had primary language impairments and included the deaf, receptive aphasics, certain severely mentally retarded persons, and autistic children. The last two groups were assumed to have all of the basic linguistic abilities and to have learned the language but were hampered in communication at the motor level only. The nonvocal group could not produce intelligible speech and the nonwriting group could neither handle a pencil nor move accurately enough for adequate communication via a guarded keyboard on an electric typewriter. Many categories of such persons were considered, but I based my figure on the estimate of nonvocal, nonwriting cerebral palsied children alone. This was assumed to be upward of 100,000 (incidence) but did not specify severity of handicap except as it affected vocal or written communication. It must be stressed that these figures were not extrapolated from hard statistics, but were based on roughly estimated percentages of nonvocalness in equally roughly known total incidence figures of each clinical condition considered. More exact figures are simply not known at present.

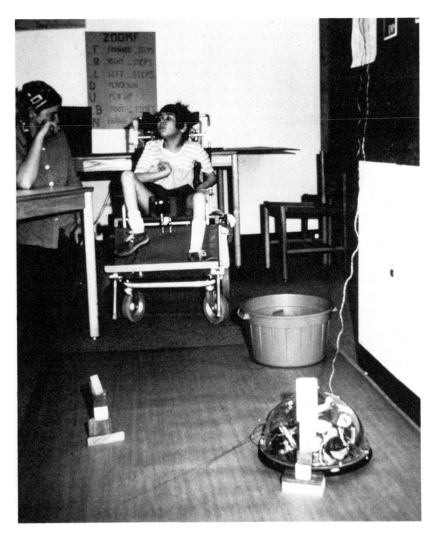

Figure 1.   Jane with robot turtle.

Such jobs as editing, computer programming, reading specimens in a pathology lab and interpreting results, coding information from a slide for a computer, and being a reference librarian all require sensitivity, thought, and personal expertise, but they are not as dependent on the speed of the worker's output as they are on the competence of the worker's judgments. Radical experiments in work environment design must be attempted.

THE EXPERIMENTS

In this text I describe a number of preliminary experiments that I conducted in the Logo group at the Massachusetts Institute of Technology (M.I.T.) and I make frequent reference to the CARIS Project (Geoffrion and Bergeron, 1978) at the University of New Hampshire.

The idea of using LOGO[4] for the physically handicapped was mentioned in a proposal made by the Logo Group in The Artificial Intelligence Laboratory of M.I.T. (Papert, 1973). Some of the work presented here that involves cerebral palsied children is part of the research conducted under that proposal. The use of Logo turtles as educational toys for autistic children was first mentioned in the literature by Weir and Emanuel (1976), who reported on one child with whom they had worked for seven sessions. The investigations reported in this book involve fewer contact hours per subject, but cover a large number of subjects, some of which were much more severely handicapped than the Weir and Emanuel case. The work of these subjects also draws attention to new phenomena. The use and implications of LOGO for deaf children are mentioned here for the first time.

Six distinct contacts with the Logo environment are described herein. Nancy and Kevin (Chapter 5) were the first special students to work on the system and were brought from a public day school in New York that is designed to meet the needs of children with moderate to severe learning or behavioral problems. The school administrators were interested in developing a Logo environment for their use, and they brought three children

---

[4]LOGO is a procedurally oriented programming language designed to be easily learnable by children and powerful enough to write sophisticated systems and artificially intelligent programs. Initial development of the language was done by Bolt Beranek and Newman, Inc. (BBN) in Cambridge, Massachusetts, and the particular system I used was significantly extended and evolved at M.I.T. The M.I.T. implementation runs on a PDP11/45 computer under a time-sharing system developed specifically for the purposes of the Logo group. The system supports four unintelligent graphic terminals capable of high-speed animation and four other printing terminals. Although the power and flexibility of the LOGO language greatly facilitated the work described in this book, most of the experiments could have been conducted with suitable equipment and some inconvenience in languages such as FORTRAN or BASIC. The main disadvantage of these other languages is their relative clumsiness, both for learning and in use, an ultimate source of frustration when the object is to teach people who do not elect to be programmers, for example handicapped children, to invent or to modify their own computer-controlled environment. Only references to the LOGO language, itself, and not to the Logo Group, the Logo turtle (a computer controlled robot), or the "Logo environment," show the word "LOGO" in upper case.

for a 2-day period to observe their reactions to our system. Nancy remained involved for the morning and afternoon sessions of both days (approximately 2 hours per session), but Kevin was sick the second day and was able to attend only on the first day.

Jane and Johnny (first mentioned in Chapter 2) and Jay (Chapter 6) were part of a group of children brought to M.I.T. from the Crotched Mountain Center at the beginning of April, 1976. All three are severely involved cerebral palsied children, and Jay and Jane have generally been thought to be retarded. After their first day's experience with Logo, it was decided that they should come down regularly, every Friday, for the remainder of the school year. Transportation problems and vacation schedules prevented this, but they did return two more times. In early June, Ellen Hildreth and I, aided at times by other members of the Logo group, brought robot turtles, terminals, and adaptive equipment to Crotched Mountain Center for a week. It was at that time that Susan and Ricky (Chapter 3), Phillip and Peter (Chapter 4), and Joey and Annette (Chapter 5) became involved in the program. Unfortunately, I had only one opportunity to work with Joey. Susan and Ricky each had two sessions with the computer, but I describe only the first session in this book. Annette dropped in on us twice spontaneously with a friend, but when time was reserved specifically for her, she was too scared, and refused to do anything but watch another child. Phillip and Peter each spent several sessions with the computer. Phillip followed us around the Center, helping us set up the equipment and using it whenever it was not otherwise scheduled.

Another Logo contact included Thomas's visit to the laboratory (Chapter 5). Three severely behaviorally disturbed children were brought to the laboratory for a day, but only Thomas is described here.

Experiences from brief contacts that my colleagues at Bolt Beranek and Newman and I made with six children at the Boston College Campus School are incorporated in the analyses, but none of these children is described individually.

The CARIS Project data and videotapes were supplied to me by Leo Geoffrion for use in this book. Reports of some of that work were appropriate to mention as an illustration of a slightly different approach to using computers with handicapped children. The important difference between CARIS and Logo, for the sake of this writing, is that CARIS has the development of reading skills as a specific goal for its activities and has a planned curriculum to lead toward that goal. The CARIS curriculum was designed by Geoffrion, and the program was implemented in FORTRAN on a PDP11/30 by Bergeron (Geoffrion and Bergeron, 1978).

Students working with the CARIS program are able to select various pictures and various animations that the pictures can perform by pointing to the English words that name the objects and actions with a special electronic "pen." After a noun is selected, its picture appears on a TV-like display screen along with a list of verbs. When the child selects a verb, the two-word sentence is displayed (e.g., DOG JUMPS) and then the cartoon is animated on the screen. Gordon's first session with the CARIS system is described in Chapter 4. Work in a similar vein is being done by Withrow (1978).

The major emphasis in this discussion is placed on the effects that are visible in the first 20 minutes of a child's first contact with the computer system. This emphasis is partly a result of the newness of these studies, and also is deliberately selected even in several of the cases where children had spent more time with the machines. The "long" contacts were never long enough to allow intelligent inferences to be made about the long-range applicability of these approaches to work with the children, and they shed no new light on the interactions between the children and us or on the equipment and the methods. However, these short contacts raised some very interesting questions, often in the first few minutes. For example, Susan (see Chapter 3) had been thought to be moderately retarded and had not been known to be a reader. In a very short time she mastered the effect of several written computer commands and executed a complex drawing task. We need no statistical tests of significance — the idea, plan, method, and execution were all her own, and it is implausible to attribute the result to accident. Considering the understanding and planning that are necessary for accomplishment of this task, it is difficult to maintain the image of Susan as moderately retarded.

Videotapes and computer transcripts of the Logo work were kept wherever possible. Approximately 8 hours of videotape were made over the course of approximately 80 contact hours with the various children.

Chapter 2
Normal Needs and
Special Needs

NORMAL NEEDS

A Budding Mozart

Whatever it means to say that a person has the "potential" to be a musical composer, it is certainly clear that in order to develop, the person's mind needs opportunities not only for stimulation and activity, but also for *feedback* from its activity. The musical ideas that reside in that mind must be examined, refined, and extended if they are to generate or to give way to new musical ideas.

The assumption that a person has a musical mind is never made a priori. We always have some evidence of it. Perhaps it is first seen in the baby's dancing, or in the older child's faithful reproduction of a song. Sometimes it must await a more sophisticated communication, such as interest and facility in playing an instrument. We do not suspect someone of a talent for composing unless he already has the performance ability to show it. When the talent is discovered, the usual course of its development includes a protracted period of skills acquisition. Some music teachers incorporate composition experiences early in a child's musical education, but performance skills remain the basics, without which there can be no feedback. During this time, as every young musician knows, one spends much time and effort preparing to play great music, less time actually playing any, and little or no time composing.

Thus, we don't find out anything about the student's talent for composing music until rather late in his training. More to the point, neither does the student. Such extensive preparation before being certain of one's interests can be a bad business investment. Some former children are thankful that their parents forced them through this stage; others are not.

A Budding Anybody

As a teacher, I want to help my students develop autonomy. I am acutely aware that this goal is not achieved merely by offering them choices and options. Unless the child can *act* on the choices and unless the choices have significantly different consequences, merely *having* the choices cannot be meaningful.

The problem is that there are many options that a 7-year-old mind is capable of inventing, wanting, and even understanding but that the 7-year-old body is totally unready for. Examples abound. One child wants to experiment with music, yet he is unable to do so without musical skills. Another child is interested in planets and planetary orbits, but he lacks the mathematical skills for looking abstractly at time and motion and lacks the physical skills and equipment to do much "playing" with the subject matter, other than copying from books. He is much more handicapped in what he can do than in what he can think about doing. A third child understands the principle behind an animated cartoon and has a clever "flip-book" cartoon idea living in his head, but he doesn't have the patience to make hundreds of nearly identical drawings or the skill to make drawings that please him and do justice to the original idea. Thus it is not only musical creativity, but all creative work that is put off by seemingly interminable preparation and exercises.

The point, of course, is not to ignore skills acquisition, but to stimulate curiosity, intellectual growth, and love for learning by providing exciting applications of these skills as they are acquired rather than waiting for the acquisition of a large number of skills. The computer as servant can make this possible.

THE COMPUTER MEETING NORMAL NEEDS — TWO METAPHORS

The Computer as Entertainer

It is a common observation that computer programmers who have access to their machines after hours will often spend those extra hours, even after a full day's work, teaching the machine "tricks." They will teach it how to play tic-tac-toe or to simulate a rocket that the user is trying to land on the moon. They will teach it to play some friendly joke on a co-worker or to print Snoopy pictures on the line printer, and they will also bring their children to play with the marvelous toy. It is remarkable that this kind of playful and creative overtime is put in by programmers almost regardless of how much or how little they otherwise like their jobs.

What is it about this toy that is so engaging? Perhaps it is the power to make it do one's bidding. Perhaps it is the opportunity to be involved in an otherwise inaccessible activity, such as landing a rocket on the moon. Perhaps it is the access to artistic creativity without having to have the artist's hands. Perhaps it is the challenge of solving tic-tac-toe so thoroughly that one can create an infallible playmate. Perhaps it is just the spirit of programming that regards nonworking programs not as failures, but as unfinished products — things that can be fixed.

The Computer as Assistant

The problems of the budding anybody seem not to exist during the computer programmer's game time. How can we put the power, opportunity, creative freedom, challenge, and spirit of computer programming in the hands of a young child?

To avoid pinning everything on another protracted skills acquisition period, we must first develop a powerful computer language that a young child can easily learn. We must also consider how the computer should respond to the child. If the computer can only print for the child, a child who does not enjoy reading is restricted in what he can do. But suppose the computer can also control a robot. The child can teach the robot how to wander about on the floor, making a drawing of its path, or to run an obstacle course, or to knock over a tower of blocks, or to escape from a maze. Suppose the computer has a high-resolution graphics display and high-speed animation capabilities. Then it can make drawings on a TV screen at the child's instruction. By teaching the computer how to make the right drawings and when and where to display them on the TV screen, the child can create original animated cartoons.

Computers can also generate musical tones, allowing the child to compose music or sound effects to accompany his cartoon. The child can narrate the cartoon with printed captions. Computer-generated speech is now inexpensive enough to be widely practical, permitting spoken narrations. A machine so outfitted can provide an unusually rich medium for language arts teaching.

The existence of speech production and speech recognition devices means that nonreading children have better opportunities than ever before to communicate with the computer. A child can speak commands to the computer and listen for those computer responses that are not overt actions. Another way for the nonreading child to communicate with the computer is by pressing buttons coded with pictures.

Lest the reader feel this to be strictly economic fantasy, it should be pointed out that all of the following capabilities — the computer with keyboard and color TV graphics; the robot device, which can be controlled by the computer and which can draw with pen on paper; the ability to speak out loud; the ability to learn, recognize, and respond to a few dozen spoken words; the ability to generate musical tones in a wide range of durations and pitches specified by the user; the ability to print messages on paper; and floppy disc mass storage — can be bought off the shelf today for less than $4,000. In the future, more capabilities will cost less.

Design and development of such computer environments for normal children have been pursued by private industry as well as by university research groups, including BBN, Xerox Corporation, Texas Instruments, and the Massachusetts Institute of Technology. The appeal of this research is perhaps best exemplified by the current proliferation of electronic games and toys.

SPECIAL NEEDS

Certain technologies can reduce the normal child's learning handicaps. These same computer environments can be tailored to the physically handicapped user. Although there is considerable room for clever improvements in the practicality, ease, and bandwidth of communication and control, all of the really fundamental problems of making it possible for a severely physically handicapped, nonvocal person to control a computer have already been solved (Luster and Vanderheiden, 1974). It is certainly not obvious that such a person need be any more handicapped at musical composition or architectural design than you or I once the problems of output and feedback are eliminated.

The computer must be fairly flexible if it is to provide full communication for the severely physically impaired child. Expressive communication requires more than speech and writing. We give travel directions with our hands, hum parts of tunes, and draw pictures and maps to help make our words clearer. When we speak, we rely so heavily on our facial expressions, verbal pauses, and vocal inflections that direct transcriptions of casually spoken messages are often extremely difficult to comprehend. Our written language is full of punctuation, underlinings, and formal wordings in an attempt to replace the information that we normally convey without words, but not even body language and gesture complete the picture.[5] We also communicate with our environment by acting upon it. Often these actions serve important interpersonal communication purposes. Without at least some voluntary motor control, there can be no communication.[6] Without fully intact motor coordination and volitional movement, some expressive communications will be impaired.

The deaf child's communication handicap slows down both input and feedback in English. Among those children fortunate enough to have been educated with sign language, the majority did not have it introduced

---

[5]It is interesting to note that the total communication movement, which is the dominant philosophy of those who advocate the use of sign language in the education of deaf children, seems not to take note of the difficulties of visual transmission of English, whose natural modality, both historically and developmentally within each hearing person, is auditory. The simultaneous presentation of spoken English and sign and the overwhelming popularity of strictly English-based sign systems force signing to proceed along the rules of English and do not make full use of the spatial and temporal structures that the manual modality makes possible and which are used in the American Sign Language (ASL). Fant's (1974) argument that ASL may be the best language for the deaf child has not been taken seriously enough. guage for the deaf child has not been taken seriously enough.

[6]"Voluntary motor control" can be any voluntarily controllable and measurable efferent, and need not be a coordinated movement.

to them as early as the hearing child's shared language began. Thus, even with sign language, we are handicapped in our ability to transmit to the child as complex an idea as he is capable of producing and manipulating in his head, but we can provide such a child with a computer environment in which the linguistic complexities are greatly reduced. The child can then begin to generate his own intellectually exciting and challenging problems and can thus explore his cognitive and educational frontiers without always having to mediate that experience through his weakest link.

Some preliminary observations suggest that the deaf child may have special abilities in certain kinds of spatial thinking. It is instructive to realize that his sign language has accustomed him to carving meaning out of space and has not so strictly constrained him to linearity, as English does. Thus, in this area, his "handicap" is certainly irrelevant and may actually be an asset. The concern is to begin seeing what the child is especially capable of, rather than focusing on what he is incapable of doing.

The notion of a prosthetic device seems, at first, less apt when applied to the autistic child, but recall the above examples. Although the deaf child can deal with verbally mediated situations, he is certainly not at his best using that medium. The physically handicapped child is at a disadvantage when he must mediate interaction with the world through coordinated motor activity. In each case, when we bypass or ignore the weak communication modality, we see very fast and exciting changes in the child. Similarly, the autistic child is often not at his best when his contact with the world has to be mediated through normal human communication or copying behavior from people. He is much better able to initiate activities than to copy them and he needs to have consistent meaning assigned to his behaviors.

It might well be a good route to communication with people for the autistic child to have an orderly computer world at first. Simple machines, such as phonographs and small mechanical toys, are often very attractive to the autistic child, but they seldom offer rich enough possibilities to expand the child's world. At the very least, learning how to communicate with a computer teaches that consistent communication is possible. My recent work and the work of others (Colby, 1973; Weir and Emanuel, 1976) shows that the computer experience can catalyze spontaneous communicative efforts, bridging the gap to human communication.

Serious abnormalities in sensation, perception, cognition, or motor control are handicaps in themselves, but they also restrict communication and give rise to secondary handicaps. It is artificial to discuss these effects as if they were separate and distinct, but the communication breakdown alone makes a grave impact on a person's life. When the information we receive from any source is incomplete, unclear, ambiguous, or contradictory, our comprehension of our situation suffers and our responses become inadequate or inappropriate, further weakening communication.

Expressive and receptive aspects of communication keep each other in tune. Although I question the popular notion that all learning requires activity, there can be little doubt about the advantages that a complete feedback loop from active involvement has over "passive" observation of the environment. Any of the handicaps I have mentioned alter or reduce the feedback loop.

From this point of view, the special needs of handicapped children may be even more striking than we had supposed. In the same way that we are handicapped in our ability to experiment with music, a child whose problems in motor control prevent him from talking, writing, or typing is handicapped in his ability to experiment with language. If the development of our musical imagination and creativity depends on its use and, in particular, our feedback from its use, we can see how devastating the lack of linguistic feedback may be to a child. Mental development in general seems to suffer functional retardation when a person can never try out his ideas and get feedback from the trials.

For the autistic, deaf, or cerebral palsied child, whose autonomy is even more limited than that of the normal child, the computer provides a tool for creative activity. Because it enables these special children to affect and control their world, and because it is a tool with which they can become proficient and show off their creativity, it offers them a powerful chance to develop their own feelings of self worth and to see themselves as learners and doers. For us it provides a clear window into the child's mind. As it enables us to see more clearly into his thinking and creating, it serves not only to aid assessment, but to deepen our understanding of the child.

THREE WAYS COMPUTERS CAN BE USED IN EDUCATION

The Computer as Tutor

Perhaps the most common nonbookkeeping use of the computer in education is as a private tutor. A program is designed by teachers and programmers to lead a child through a sequence of steps to learn some desired behavior. Although the child may be an active member of the child-computer team, it is the child who is being programmed. The interaction is guided by the computer, which generally initiates all of the transactions (poses a problem, asks a question, or gives an instruction) and chooses its next course of action based on the child's response to the last one.

Proponents of this use of the computer argue that the computer, unlike a person, is available, untiring, patient, able to keep detailed and flawless records, and able to juggle those records to choose the smoothest path for the student's learning based on past and current performance.

This use of the computer develops out of what I call the *hospital model* of educational intervention. Students are tested, screened, and diagnosed. Weaknesses are identified and programs of remediation are prescribed. This model is prevalent even in settings where the most immediately visible and preemptive characteristic of the children is not some severe handicap.

Serious risks attend this model. Although perhaps practical for certain academic skill goals, computerized programmed learning streamlines an aspect of teaching that properly constitutes only a tiny fraction of the business in which students and teachers ought to be engaged. Moreover, it assumes, a priori, that the child is not the agent, but the patient. Thus, whenever our goal for a child is to build his autonomy and initiative, this model is counterproductive. At the best, progress toward autonomy is superficial; at the worst, it is undermined altogether.[7] For the handicapped person, the hospital model is a superfluous reminder of his own disabilities.

The Computer as Eyeglasses

Unlike a tutor, eyeglasses have no agenda for the wearer. They contain no information for the wearer to learn and they do not try to teach, yet they allow the wearer to do things that would otherwise be difficult, perhaps impossible. The computer allows a child to make an animated cartoon without requiring that he have the drawing skill in his hands, and to experiment with musical ideas without requiring that he first gain competence at an instrument. The computer extends and amplifies the abilities of the person with normal needs. Again, one sees the same (and more) vast possibilities for people who have special needs.

The important distinction between the tutor metaphor and the eyeglasses metaphor is the shift of emphasis from programming oneself to

---

[7]Weir and Emanuel (1976) refer to the passive pupil role and the emotionally committed role of their autistic student, David. When David was being taught, when the agenda was not his and the activities were not thoroughly within his control, he "acted autistic" and assumed the passive role. When he was the agent, the researchers observed increases in appropriate spontaneous speech, improvements in vocal tone, changes in body posture signifying interest and involvement, and obvious pleasure.

learning how to influence one's surroundings — from focusing inward to focusing outward.

The Computer as Mirror

A device that can sense extremely slight variations in an act we perform and that can be programmed to recognize the fine distinctions between relevant and irrelevant variations can be used to provide very sensitive feedback on our performance. For example, a machine that draws distinctly different pictures depending on our pronunciation of a vowel can give more accurate feedback than our untrained (or deaf) ear can, and thus it can guide us to correct pronunciation (Nickerson and Stevens, 1973; Nickerson, Kalikow, and Stevens, 1976). A device capable of identifying muscular activity even before we have been able to muster the strength or coordination to produce a visible movement can tell us when we are addressing the correct muscles. It will be easier to consider the applications of this kind of technology if I describe them in relation to a particular child who might benefit from them.

> Jane is a 13-year-old, spastic, cerebral palsied girl whose size and physical development make her appear to be about 9 years of age. Her voluntary movement (arms, legs, and mouth) is extremely restricted in speed, range, accuracy, and strength. She cannot sit herself up in bed, dress, feed herself, or control her wheelchair. She has a reflex grasp, but for practical use, she cannot grasp or hold anything. On occasion, she speaks, but she seldom produces more than a high squeak. She has signs for "yes" and "no," and, slowly and with great effort, she can point to words on her word board. Within the limitations of her ability to respond, Jane shows that she can read, spell (including reasonable spelling for new words), arrange words in grammatical order, and understand spoken language. Her medical records show disagreement about her mental capability, some diagnosticians claiming she is retarded and others referring to her as a "bright little girl."

Jane's physical abilities vary considerably from day to day, with motivation apparently a key factor. This is perhaps not very surprising when we consider the payoffs Jane receives for her efforts. The mark of real autonomy depends on what options are open to the individual. For a child whose movements are uncoordinated but stronger than Jane's, showing independence by doing as much as possible without help might be the clearest sign of autonomy. For Jane, however, there is no independence to show. There is nothing of real salience in her life that she can do completely alone, so all of her efforts only serve to help the person she is dependent on. Thus, the greatest show of her autonomy, paradoxically, is to do less than she is capable of, to withhold the help that she can give, to use her own dependency to control others. The discrepancies between her best performances and her typical performance are great. Some people make generous allowances, but others say she is obstinate, lazy, or even a deliberate con artist. The interpretations vary, but the observations are the same; she seems unmotivated and does less than she appears capable of.

In order to give Jane appropriate care, we must consider both her physical abilities and her psychological state, her motivation. In school she appears not to use her word board unless coerced into it. Being the first to respond "Tuesday" when asked in class what day yesterday was is not a driving life issue for her. The major problem that she faces is that, if people left her, she could not live at all. For Jane, making a living consists not of academics, but of keeping people nearby who have taken physical care of her and whom she likes. Pointing to "kiss" or "thank you" or "I like you" in the latter context is something she does, apparently quite readily. If one follows the line of thinking still further, it costs Jane effort to communicate, and the returns should be great if we expect her to make the investment. With a sufficiently friendly computer interface she could turn on or off a TV at will, drive her own wheelchair, and select from and eventually create her own computer entertainments. The addition of efficient, useful, and satisfying communication to her life may have an avalanche of benefits.

INFORMATION, SELF-EXPRESSION, AND FEEDBACK

The most obvious limitation of a child like Jane is her inability to do the things we take for granted, such as walking, riding a bicycle, playing with dolls, or doodling on paper. However, it is not merely the activities that Jane misses, but the information (perceptual, academic, and social) that those activities afford. We are not yet sophisticated enough in our understanding of human learning to state precisely the impact of such informal learning, but it is obvious that this kind of learning is certainly normal. Further, textbook writers and curriculum designers, even for the special child, tacitly assume that the student in school has had a vast wealth of out-of-school experiences to draw upon. It is so difficult to imagine not having had all of the normal experiences — in fact, we are so totally unaware of them that it is difficult even to list them — that we may frequently interpret a handicapped child's failure to comprehend as a lack of intellectual capacity rather than as a fundamental lack of information.

A second problem that is commonly the focus of considerable attention is the child's expressive language handicap. The inability to write or to type, even for a child who is able to speak easily, has a grave impact on the child's learning. Although the child can and does constantly learn from what he sees and hears around him, the specific relationship of teacher and student requires that both parties get adequate feedback on their interaction. The child who cannot produce a written response must orally express his comprehension (or lack thereof) of a principle of physics, his impressions of a book, or even his ability to add. Some skills are almost unlearnable in the absence of writing.[8]

If the nonwriting child also cannot speak — or does so only with difficulty — he is almost totally ruled out of conventional teacher-student relationships. When a teacher can get only a yes/no response, a few crude gestures, and a limited amount of unreliable pointing, there is seldom enough information available to guide the teaching/learning process. Thus, the physically handicapped child, who has already been deprived of much of the incidental "sandbox learning" (nonschool) experiences of the normal child, may lose the chance to learn efficiently even in the classroom for lack of appropriate feedback, regardless of the child's intellectual capacity.

What is physically wrong with Jane is her motor handicap, but the secondary problems arising from such severely restricted expressive ability and limited feedback so totally overshadow the "original" problem that they must be considered the real handicap. By the time she had reached school age, her experiences had been so abnormal for so long that the development of communication was no longer a "simple" matter of providing a modality and teaching the academic skills. Her life-style had not required verbal communication and had specifically adapted to its absence. Even the English input that she received was not normal. Conversational behavior is a highly structured activity that breaks down when one side is not responding normally. People tend to talk to an expressively handicapped child less often, less intelligently, and about a far more limited range of things than they would with a normal child. For Jane to become competent at being a nonvocal, nonambulatory, nonmanipulative adolescent, she must learn to satisfy her needs without text production capabilities (for a common example). Furthermore, her experiences rarely give her much to say. A communication aid provides her only with the modality and not with a reason to communicate. Worse yet, it allows us to be deceived about her capabilities. If she can communicate but does not, or if she can, but does so "defectively," or if she can and we use that modality to test her and she tests poorly, we may (and frequently do) falsely assume her to be intellectually lacking.

---

[8]Perhaps the most elementary example of this is multi-digit multiplication. This cannot be performed in the way it is almost universally taught in American elementary schools unless one writes the partial products or develops a phenomenal memory.

Motoric disability thus eliminates many direct experiences that the child could have. It distorts or destroys many of the vicarious experiences that fluent communication could provide, but even this is not the full extent of the destruction that a severe physical handicap can produce. The child's perceptual development itself may be below that of an able-bodied child. Considerable research suggests that perceptual development depends at least to some extent on perceptual-motor mapping that develops out of observing (and otherwise sensing) one's own coordinated activity. (Note that some of the experiences with handicapped children reported here raise questions about this theory.) Presumably, this means that even if we were able to perform just the right surgery to "fix" the nervous system of the nonvocal, spastic-athetoid quadriplegic, such an individual would still have to learn how to walk, to draw, to catch a ball, and to talk.

WHERE TO FOCUS: BEHAVIOR OR EXPERIENCE

Typically, efforts at habilitating the handicapped have focused on normalizing behavior rather than on normalizing experience. When we lacked the technology to adapt an environment to a child, then we often had no other choice than to focus only on adapting the child to his environment. When a child's motor control was poor, then the primary goal, sometimes despite considerable pain to ourselves and the child, was to improve it. Despite the worthiness of motor control as an end in itself, it is for most of us simply a means to the real goal of a full, rich, and satisfying life. The effort a child must put out to improve a physical skill is generally extremely hard to motivate unless the child can see some clear sign that the effort will pay off. An emphasis on patching the child is beneficial only as long as it is pursued with enough patience not to cause more frustration than growth and, more importantly, as long as some interim way for the child to regain and develop his autonomy is fostered — and, of course, only so long as real improvement is regularly seen.

The two different orientations — patching the child to normalize behavior or patching the environment to normalize experience — significantly affect the way in which one deals with the handicapped child. If we try to normalize the communication behavior of the deaf child, for example, we stress the development of speech more than the development of sign language. If, on the other hand, we aim to make the deaf child's communication experience more like that of the normal child, we try to provide him with a fluent and easy communication system — more likely sign language than speech. In my view, it is the child's abnormal experience of the world (e.g., his lack of easy, fluent communication and casual play) more than his abnormal behavior (e.g., his inability to speak, write, or walk) that handicaps the child.

An attempt at synthesizing these two orientations can be seen in schools where sign is the accepted communication means but where oral skills are heavily emphasized. While some synergy of the two approaches might be hoped for, it would depend on the transferability of language skills from one modality to another, a transfer that cannot be taken for granted. With care, however, an approach designed to normalize experience may directly serve to normalize behavior as well.

Another way of seeing the two approaches just mentioned is through the different models of therapeutic intervention. I call one the *exercise model* and the other the *substitution model*. The exercise model concentrates on functional habilitation (normalizing behavior). In the area of communication, speech therapy generally follows an exercise model. The substitution model provides alternative means of communication, such as scanning communicators, headsticks, and word boards.[9] Despite the concurrence of these two approaches, I feel that there has been an inadequate synthesis of their purposes and that available technology now makes that synthesis practical.

Consider these two models as they apply to a nearsighted person whose vision prevents him from reading normal text. Exercises might start by having this person read very large print and then gradually replacing it with smaller and smaller print until, we hope, the person can successfully read normal typewriter print. Alternatively, fearing that this may never actually succeed, we might teach the person to read Braille and to use a white cane! The goal of returning good function to the eyes in the first instance is frustrated in part by the difficulty of the task and in part by the sacrifices that the individual must make along the way, namely, not being able to read anything but the practice material. In the second instance, however, it is reasonable to suppose that the person will miss some useful opportunities to maintain his vision and will, in effect, let his vision atrophy.

Of course, we have the technology that synthesizes these two approaches: eyeglasses. Glasses provide immediate access to reading and keep the eyes useful in the process. They neither give up on the weak system nor require protracted exercise periods before any functional use. By providing support to a system which, although well developed, cannot stand alone, glasses restore essentially normal status to a person who would be severely disabled without them.

---

[9]All of these replace vocal expression. Some substitute nonvocal representations of English, while others dispense with English altogether.

The central point being made here is that our programs must be enriching rather than restricting. Most behavior-oriented therapy, and almost all of computer-aided instruction, has focused on training specific behaviors for specific circumstances and eliminating unwanted behaviors. Sometimes "abnormal" behaviors have been recklessly extinguished without any consideration for the adaptive and useful functions they were performing. (For an interesting analysis of this problem, see Prizant, 1978). Since we cannot always know what value a behavior pattern has, we can best serve the human being who comes to us for help by trying to remove the barriers to his experiences, thus making room for him to develop his own adaptive and integrative abilities — room for him to develop autonomy.

Part II
Special Children

Chapter 3
Cerebral Palsy, Motor Experience, and Cognitive Development

THE CHILDREN

Susan

Susan is 16 years old, quadriplegic, and generally assumed to be mildly retarded. Her speech is limited, but improving. Prior to her work with the computer, she had no experience with communication boards. She can feed herself slowly and can type using her right hand and a guarded keyboard. Her reading and arithmetic are both at a primary grade level. Her low level of language skills makes it difficult for her to show much intellectual ability verbally, and her physical difficulties and motivational difficulties make nonverbal assessment equally unreliable.

When Susan first saw the equipment on her ward, she wanted to try it out, but she had to wait, partly because there were already other children working with it and partly because the equipment that would allow a person with physical disabilities as severe as hers to operate it successfully was not working properly at the time. Susan watched the equipment whenever she had the chance. By the time her turn came, she had already seen the robot turtle move around on the floor and had heard parts of my explanation about how to move it.

We had no adequate guard for the computer terminal keyboard and could not use a video display over the telephone lines, so we brought a flatbed plotter with us to use as a command-scanning communicator for children like Susan.

Such plotters are usually used for drawing figures or graphs, but all we wanted it to do was point at items on three heirarchical lists of commands. The left-most list (see Figure 2) contained the ''top level'' choices for Susan, including the ringing of a BELL (for attention or help), selecting another WORD BOARD (menu of lists), composing and playing computer-generated MUSIC, controlling the robot TURTLE, and moving the scanner FASTER or SLOWER.

The pen on the plotter scanned past each element of this list, pausing for about 1.5 seconds at each entry, giving Susan enough time to select the item if she chose to. To select an item, she struck the terminal keyboard anywhere with her hand or elbow. The plotter would respond with a click to verify that the computer had recognized her choice and then the appropriate action would be taken. In this case (Figure 2), she selected TURTLE and the plotter/scanner moved to the right to scan the second list, a list of commands to the turtle.

The turtle can be instructed to go FORWARD a specific number of steps in the direction it is heading. To choose a number, Susan had to select NUMBER, watch the plotter scan the third column and select the

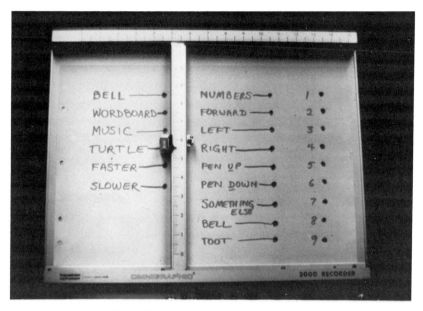

Figure 2.   A makeshift command-scanner.

number she wanted. The plotter would then immediately return to the second column to find out how to use the number, whether it was intended as the number of steps FORWARD, the number of degrees to change heading RIGHT or LEFT, or the number of times to TOOT. Offered the choice of either making the turtle draw for her or using it to knock down a tower, she chose to draw, and she commanded the turtle to put its PEN DOWN. Had she chosen SOMETHING ELSE, Susan would have caused the scanner to return to the top level (left hand) column.

I had been told that Susan could not read the particular words that were on the list of commands and so, at first, I read each command as the pointer pointed to it. I was not thinking much about what the turtle was drawing and assumed that her initial play was essentially without a plan. Having chosen the largest number for both the turtle's distance forward and the turtle's turn to the right, Susan made three lines — a long line starting near her and going away ("north"), followed by a very sharp turn to the right (facing the turtle "southeast"), another long line, the same sharp turn to the left (facing the turtle "north" again), and a third line.

I remarked that she had drawn an N, the initial of her last name. Whether this had been her plan all along or a new idea, I do not know, but she seemed very pleased at my comment.

She then had me move the turtle far off to the left of the N. After selecting a smaller number to shorten the distance that the turtle would go forward each time, she began drawing again. At first, I thought she was going to make a smaller N, because she left the angles the same. She made a design using four short lines with the same sharp angle between them and then diminished the angle through which the turtle would turn. It became apparent that the design before she changed the angle was a false start as she systematically made short lines and gentle turns, turning first to the left and then later to the right to draw an S. Her initials — SN! The total time from her alleged inability to read the commands to the completion of her surely planned and sophisticated task was about 30 minutes.

Ricky

Ricky is 12 years old, and has never had speech or any functional use of his limbs. He is quite obviously very bright and has been able to show his intelligence easily. He has good head control and can type well with a headstick. Academic skills are all excellent and it has been a challenge to his teachers and therapists to find things Ricky can do with such an active mind and such an inactive body.

Ricky wanted to draw with the floor turtle. We had it set up on a table so that it would be easier for him to see as he typed instructions to it. I quickly explained the various conventions of typing to a computer — how one can correct errors, how one ends a command, and how literal-minded a computer is. Ricky began typing as I was explaining things. As he struck a key, I would echo back to him what he had done, since our equipment made it impossible for him both to type and to see what he was typing.

He made several turns in both directions with the turtle and varied the angles considerably. When he tried the FORWARD command, the distances he typed were always very small, barely perceptible. I explained that FORWARD 50 would move the turtle about an inch and suggested he might like to try something in the hundreds. He made some more turns and faced the turtle toward himself, as I continued to suggest that he try some forward move.

Why was I so impatient? He was setting the turtle up. He typed the FORWARD command, and as he typed the distance, I echoed back "Six. Sixty. Six-hundred?" He had a very contained smile as he typed yet another zero and hit the carriage return. Ricky's smile broadened when I echoed, "Six-thousand?!! I better get over there to catch the turtle as it dives off the table!" As the turtle approached the edge of the table, he laughed out loud. I asked him if I should turn it around and put it back on the table; he nodded "yes."

Whether or not he actually did figure it out before trying the experiment, I do not know, but Ricky's arithmetic is very good and he could easily have calculated that FORWARD 6000 would drive the turtle 10 feet. Anyway, his joke required me to catch the turtle at the other end of the table and turn it around again, which brought another good laugh from Ricky. His satisfaction with the whole event was apparent when the turtle finally stopped for good and he just kept looking at it and smiling. Shortly afterward, he typed a message saying that he wanted to type a letter to his family about the computer.

What opportunities to experiment with distance or angle does a person with the physical limitations of Ricky or Susan really have? How much opportunity is there for any child to do a real experiment with large numbers?

THE THEORISTS — COGNITIVE
DEVELOPMENT DEPENDS ON ACTIVITY

One of the most widely accepted theories about intellectual growth holds that early motor development is the root of all cognitive development. The versions of this theory vary slightly with each proponent, but all make the plausible assumption that each new cognitive achievement is built onto the solid foundation of those that preceded it, ultimately depending on the earliest cognitive achievement: voluntary motor activity.

Bruner — Enactive, Iconic, Symbolic — "In That Order"

Bruner (1964) has written:

> It is fruitful...to distinguish three systems of processing information by which human beings construct models of their world: through action, through imagery, and through language.... I shall call the three modes of representation...enactive representation, iconic representation and symbolic representation. *Their appearance in the life of the child is in that order, each depending upon the previous one for its development,* yet all of them remaining more or less intact throughout life — barring such early accidents as blindness or deafness or cortical injury....
> By enactive representation, I mean a mode of representing past events through appropriate *motor response.*
> We cannot, for example, give an adequate description of familiar sidewalks or floors over which we habitually walk, nor do we have much of an image of what they are like. Yet we get about them without tripping or even looking much. Such segments of our environment — bicycle riding, tying knots, as-

pects of driving — get represented in our muscles, so to speak. (pp. 1, 2; italics mine) [*Copyright 1964 by the American Psychological Association. Reprinted by permission.*]

Although these particular examples of learning all take place after the normal child has developed encoding schemes other than enactive representation, Bruner's statements make it clear that he is saying that if the child had not been able to represent "past events through appropriate motor response," then even iconic and symbolic representation would remain undeveloped.

Kephart — "The Eye Follows the Hand"

Kephart (1971) is even more explicit about the role of motor learning in the development of perception and cognition. He has stated:

> The early motor or muscular responses of the child, which are the earliest behavioral responses of the human organism, represent the beginnings of a long process of development and learning. Through these first motor explorations, the child begins to find out about himself and the world around him, and his motor experimentation and his motor learnings become the foundation upon which such knowledge is built. In early childhood, mental and physical activities are closely related, and motor activities play a major role in intellectual development. To a large extent, so-called higher forms of behavior develop out of and have their roots in motor learning. (p. 79)

Although it is not perfectly clear from this statement that Kephart believes that the motor learnings are the only possible foundation for higher forms of behavior, he is so precise about the mechanism by which cognition develops that one must conclude that he sees the early motor activity as essential. For example:

> The first processing patterns are devoted to collating perceptual data and motorical. Perception supplies the information upon which behavior is based. Motor responses supply the movements which are the overt aspects of the behavior. . . .
> Unless some relationship is established between the motor functions and the perceptual functions, the child builds up a body of perceptual information. . .but this body of perceptual information will not be related to his motor information and hence will not influence it. . . .
> The child first moves his hand and watches his hand as it moves. The hand is the actively exploring part and is producing the major part of the information. The eye follows the hand and its information is correlated with that of the hand. Thus, the eye is taught to see what the hand feels. . . .
> It is no wonder that many children in the early school grades have not yet completed the process [of integrating perceptual and motor information]. Many of our classroom presentations for such children lack meaning because they exist in only one form, not in both. They fail to eventuate in changes in

behavior because of the difficulty of the translations required. Initially the body of motor information provides the basis for the match. *Perception is matched to motor, not the reverse.* It is important that the match be made in the proper direction. (1971, p. 19 ff.; italics mine)

Kephart's theory states that, without the motor information, the child's behavior remains unaffected by perceptual data, and that these data lack meaning. Again it is clear that Kephart believes early motor learning to be an essential precursor to the rest of cognitive development.

Piaget — "Knowledge is Derived From Action"

Because "doing is the best route to understanding" is old folk wisdom, it seems wrong to point to any single source as its ultimate origin. Yet, the experimental examination of this folk wisdom with its consequent elevation to a scientific theory should probably be credited to Piaget.

> How... is the baby going to construct a world of permanent objects situated in a real space, and thus escape from his primitive egocentric universe? It is the work of the sensori-motor or practical intelligence, which precedes language, to set up a system of relations to co-ordinate this series of various perspectives which the baby has and thus cause him to locate himself among objects instead of illusively bringing them to him. In other words, as the activity of the baby develops and the causal, temporal, and spatial sequences which this activity creates become more complex, objects are detached more and more from the action itself, and the body of the subject becomes one element among others in an ordered ensemble.... The permanence of objects... depends... upon the way in which the sensori-motor or practical intelligence allows the child to free himself from his initial egocentricity.... (1937, p. 38)

More succinctly, Piaget has stated that

> Knowledge is derived from action.... To know an object is to act upon it and to transform it.... To know is therefore to assimilate reality into structures of transformation, and these are the structures that intelligence constructs as a direct extension of our actions. (1971, p. 28)

If Piaget has not been clear enough, his various redactors, popularizers, and loyal disciples go even farther. Isaacs, quoted in Hardeman, has commented

> On [sic] Piaget's view, which all the data strongly support, the activity of thinking is itself derived from the child's outward action. Indeed, it is such action, continued in another form: carried on internally and then gradually refined and developed up to the final level which Piaget calls operational. Even the most abstruse logical or mathematical operation remains for him a form of action, organically evolved from the child's first directed behaviour. (1974, p. 140)

Interpretations for Teachers

Despite Piaget's protest "I am not a pedagogue myself, and I don't have any advice to give to educators" (Evans, 1973, p. 51), educators continue to base their policies on embellishments, exaggerations, and misunderstandings of Piaget's interpretation of his research.

Ault (1977) tells us specifically how we should teach the preschool child:

> The preschool child...should be given tasks that allow him to act on objects. To learn about numbers, he should have things to count. Objects should be provided for him to touch or move as he repeats a number aloud.... To learn about colors, the child might sort colored objects, not just recite names while a teacher holds up a colored swatch. To learn shapes, he can place shapes in a form board, copy specific designs, or walk a pattern on the floor. The essential aspects are movement and acting on objects. Verbal abstractions are minimized for two reasons: they do not capture the child's attention very well and they are not active enough or concrete enough to produce learning, given the mental structures available at that level of development. (pp. 177-178)

Pulaski (1971) tells us, in the name of Piaget, that

> Children do not learn by sitting passively in their seats, listening to the teacher, any more than they learn to swim by sitting in rows on a wharf, watching grown-up swimmers in the water. (p. 197)

> The schools have been paying lip service to "learning by doing" since the days of Dewey — but most of the time it is merely a cliche. Piaget has shown us, in his thorough and painstaking studies of the child, that verbal understanding is superficial and "deforming"; learning, whether for children or their teachers, comes only through the subject's own activity. (p. 205)

Cognition Without Activity — A Puzzle

The question that arises is this: What becomes of the cognitive development of those individuals who, due to cerebral palsy or some other severely physically limiting condition, were prevented from going through the normal sensorimotor phase of development? Bruner indicates his awareness that enactive, iconic, or symbolic representation might be frustrated by "early accidents" but he indicated only that such accidents could prevent these forms of representation from "remaining...intact throughout life." We are still left with his formulation that they appear "in the life of the child...in that order, each depending upon the previous one...." If a child is born with severe neuromuscular impairment, he may be barred from reaching, grasping, rolling over, and sucking. In some cases, eye incoordination will even limit the visual tracking ability of the infant. The theories of Piaget, Kephart, and Bruner would seem to predict no alternative to severe mental retardation for a child so physically afflicted, and yet — and surely this can come as no surprise to any of the theorists — there are very severely physically handicapped persons who are cognitively quite normal (Jordan, 1972; Kopp and Shaperman, 1973).

The Meaning of Action

One way of accounting for this contradiction is to recast the theories with a somewhat softer definition of the physical action required of the infant. Perhaps one need not manipulate objects with one's hand if one can perform the same displacements and deformations with one's eyes. Perhaps shifting one's gaze and attending selectively to one's environment are sufficiently active to support the notion that actions shape the child's developing intellect. Ault (1977) seems to interpret Piaget's theory in that way.

> [The child] actively seeks certain types of stimulation and avoids others. For example, he looks at the bars of his crib rather than at the middle of his mattress. He focuses on his mother's eyes instead of on her ears. He turns his head toward the sound of his mother's voice, but he does not turn toward the window when the lawn mower passes by. (p. 12)

One problem with this formulation is that it still tacitly assumes normal sensation and voluntary control of head and eye movements. Even that amount of control is not always possible for some severely cerebral palsied infants who seem to make relatively normal cognitive progress. Another difficulty, perhaps more serious, is that the meaning of "active" has undergone a shift. When Ault says the child "actively seeks certain types of stimulation," we cannot tell if she is referring to a purely mental phenomenon or a mental phenomenon expressed in physical actions. Some of those who cite Piaget as a source are clearly referring to purely mental activity. For example, Brennan (1975, p. 463) refers to the child as being "active...in the construction of his language system." (See pp. 68–69 in Chapter 4 for Brennan's remark in context.) If mental activity can serve in place of physical activity, Piaget's original statements begin to feel genuinely vacuous. Surely, all the emphasis on physical activity was not merely to tell us that a child who is totally devoid of voluntary interaction with the world would not develop formal operations.

Research on Cognition Without Activity

One way in which we might test the theory would be to study the cognitive development of physically handicapped children. A conservative estimate indicates that there are tens of thousands of people who have no functional use of their limbs, inadequate trunk stability to roll over or raise their heads, no sucking in infancy, no speech, and even poor eye coordi-

nation. Not all of these people, perhaps very few of them, are also mentally retarded.

Estimates of the incidence of cerebral palsy are relatively easy to
come by, but census figures are not classified in ways that are useful for
computing the interaction of severity of physical limitation with cognitive
development, and there are very few studies that are in any way relevant.
Cruickshank et al. (1976b), in a section about the cognitive development
of cerebral palsied children, have stated:

> There is a relative paucity of research on the cognitive development of cere-
> bral palsied children. This is particularly surprising when one considers that
> cerebral palsied individuals, being motorically and sometimes perceptually
> handicapped, would make the ideal subjects for a testing of some of the pri-
> mary theoretical notions of psychologists like Piaget and Werner. (p. 173)

They cite only three studies, none of which comes close to settling the
issue. One of these, the Melcer and Peck (1967) study, is discussed in this
chapter. A computer search through both the ERIC and Exceptional
Child data bases turns up no other reports of related research as of May,
1978.

In the absence of information directly relevant to the issue of physical activity and cognitive development, one might look at the figures on
IQs of cerebral palsied persons as a first approximation. One study shows
that 35% of the spastic quadriplegics had IQ scores over 70, only about
1% scored over 100, and about 0.4% scored over 120 — a clear difference from the normal distribution (reviewed by Cruickshank et al.,
1976a). Less totally involved groups (such as paraplegics) had, in general,
higher IQs.

These data do not, however, support the interpretation that motor
activity is needed for cognitive growth. We might as easily explain the low
IQs in the more severely impaired individuals directly on the basis of the
brain damage that caused the motoric dysfunction or on the greater difficulty the tester has in communicating properly with the individual. In
fact, it is tempting to infer that cognitive development can proceed admir-
ably without motor functioning just on the basis of the one spastic quadriplegic whose IQ was over 150, but even there we are frustrated. The data
do not indicate how severe the spasticity was in the several high IQ quadriplegics and therefore we cannot tell how much early motor experience
they actually had.

Melcer and Peck (1967) have attempted to measure directly the effects of motoric impairment on cognitive functioning. The investigators
examined the development of action concepts in cerebral palsied children.
Among other measures, they modified the Peabody Picture Vocabulary

Test (PPVT) so that each card contained both an object representation of the vocabulary item and an action representation of the item, e.g., a ball versus someone playing with a ball.

> Cerebral palsied children are deficient in perceptual motor ability. They do not develop concepts of actions in the same ratio to object concepts as children who are not motorically handicapped. Lastly, they tend to resolve means-end situations by activity modes that involve less overt motoric action than non-cerebral palsied children. (p. 35)

> The major conclusion that can be drawn is that the results of this study support, in many ways, the currently popular theories that sensori-motor experience in infancy is one of the main factors in conceptual development... (p. 36)

This is the "major conclusion" if a conclusion can be drawn, but the authors point out themselves that problems with the testing instruments weakened their results and that it was impossible to compare the preschool treatments of the experimental and control groups. Considering how vastly the handicapped child's experiences differ from those of the normal child — not only in school but at home and not only in general learning situations, but in social, emotional, and motivational realms as well — these differences cannot be dismissed lightly.

The confusion about what would or would not support Piaget's theory is even more general than already indicated. Research with deaf children and adolescents has routinely found delays in some areas of cognitive development. To the extent that these delays might be the results of the social and intellectual isolation that come with the deaf child's communication handicap, we would expect the youngest deaf children to be least affected. In particular, if sensorimotor experiences dominate learning even after normal children have learned to understand language, perhaps we should see no early developmental delay of the deaf child's cognition. A recent study by Best and Roberts (1975) has concluded that

> These young deaf children are progressing quite normally through the sensori-motor stage of cognitive development. These results support Piaget's contention that sensori-motor development is primarily dependent on the child's active interaction with the environment. (p. 28)

Their conclusion assumes that, aside from the lack of linguistic input to the deaf group, the two groups were treated essentially the same. Even ignoring the fact that, according to the study, there were important and significant differences in the treatment that the two groups received, the results do not support their conclusion. What is supported is a contention that cognitive development, at least at the sensorimotor stage, is not dependent on (auditory) linguistic input. A study in which development progressed *normally* cannot show what that development depended on; it can, at best, indicate what was *not* essential. Several legitimate conclusions were drawn in the study, but this was not one of them.

Flavell (1977) has hypothesized

> that when it comes to acquiring certain major kinds of cognition, human beings are amazingly *versatile*. They can often make do with whatever acquisitional machinery they possess and with whatever environmental content comes their way. If the usual, typical developmental route is blocked, the child may find an unusual, atypical one that somehow gets him to at least approximately the same cognitive destination. (p. 238)

He then counterargues that

> There is a problem with these optimistic, Rousseauesque notions of developmental versatility and resiliency, however. The problem is that children do not always prove versatile and resilient in the face of organismic or environmental handicaps. . . . What we need to know, and do not yet know, is what combinations of the relevant variables result in favorable versus unfavorable developmental outcomes: what kinds of children, what kinds of handicaps, when these handicaps are incurred and when removed, and what kinds of cognitive acquisitions we are talking about. (p. 238) [*Reprinted by permission of Prentice-Hall, Inc., Englewood Cliffs, New Jersey.*]

Few people question that there is a relationship between early physical activity and intellectual development. The difficulty that remains is deciding what that relationship really is. There appear to be clear counterexamples to the theories, at least as they are expressed by Piaget. However, until recently, with the computer prosthesis, there were not sufficiently clear ways of demonstrating the independence of motor ability and intellectual ability since the efficiency of expression of the intellect depended so heavily on motoric function. Piaget's statement that "knowledge is derived from action" needs to be reexamined. If action is essential at all, the question now becomes: How much of what kind of action?

Action Without Interaction

How much of an effect must a person be able to cause voluntarily before we judge him to have interacted with his environment? As long as we live at all, we interact with the world. We consume oxygen; we convert food to waste; we give off heat. The theories of Bruner, Kephart, and Piaget, however, clearly require a much more deliberate and voluntary interaction with the world than consuming oxygen and certainly claim that such a weak interaction, alone, is insufficient to support cognitive growth.

To examine the hypothesis that cognitive development requires active motor control, we might well want to look at children who are severely disabled and see how their cognitive development has proceeded, but how shall we define "severely disabled" for the purposes of this study?

Let us consider an imaginary extreme case, a child who, from birth, has been utterly paralyzed from head to toe with the single exception that he can freely aim and focus his eyes.

If this child does not appear to show normal cognitive development, we cannot infer from this alone that the hypothesis is correct. Too many variables remain uncontrolled. To reiterate, whatever caused the paralysis (not the paralysis itself) may have interfered with cognitive development. Moreover, such a child is inevitably deprived of many normal experiences — social, emotional, and intellectual — beyond the manipulation of objects making it difficult to sort out which of these factors is responsible for the cognitive agenesis. Finally, and most significant, our inability to detect a strength does not mean it does not exist.

The alternative result — that this child does show significant cognitive growth — is more interesting. Does it suffice as a counterexample to the hypothesis? Not exactly. Eye control does not affect the environment, but perhaps that does not matter to a brain. Eye movements displace objects on the retina just as hand manipulations of those objects do. Deliberate shift of gaze is a motor activity that causes predictable sensory effects. Perhaps this pseudocontrol of the environment is sufficient to support cognitive development.

This alternative represents something of a departure from the strong and explicit positions of Bruner, Kephart, and Piaget, but it salvages the notion that active control over one's experiences is necessary for mental growth.

Can we go even further? It might be that the manipulation one produces directly with one's own muscles can be totally replaced by "remote control" manipulations performed at one's command. This could be significant if object manipulation were found to be the key to mental growth, but normal manipulative ability were precluded because of some disability.

An even more extreme case may help clarify how this could be. Let us follow the cognitive growth of an imaginary child whose only voluntary movement is the raising and lowering of his right eyebrow. The difference between this child and the one we invented before is not in their ability to be voluntarily active (they both have that ability), but in their ability to be *interactive*.

The eybrow child has no predictable effect on the environment. The only voluntary control he has is over a part of his environment from which he cannot easily get feedback. Unless the raised eyebrow were the only externally visible movement the child made (even involuntarily), it seems unlikely that even the child — not having had any obvious feedback — would know that he had that control. Using that control to signal to another person would require that the other person (not the child) notice the purposive movement, realize its potential value, and establish a code, since initially the child has no way of communicating his own choice of code or even his intent to communicate.

In principle, the eybrow child's mother could become a kind of human prosthesis for motor exploration by manipulating objects in the child's field of view according to commands eyebrowed by the child. In reality, no codes exist that an infant could use in that way, and thus such a person would inevitably spend years being totally devoid of voluntary control.

The question is whether a child who has had a history like this will show any mental development. In order to research that, we would have to provide the means by which such a child could exert fluent control over the testing materials. To put the child in control of a situation and see what happens does not require a complex code. We can condition a 1-month-old infant to suck differentially in response to particular stimuli and can thus determine his ability to distinguish degrees of variation that we might introduce (Morse, 1974). Such a technique obviously assumes no more cognitive growth than takes place normally in the first month of life and so might be deemed fair to use in our experiment. Were we to test our paralyzed imaginary eyebrow person at 12 years of age and discover only an infant's intellect, we would still have difficulty linking the infant's ability to manipulate actively and the child's cognitive development because of the very serious problems in eliminating confounding variables.

As will be better shown later, the computer is the ideal tool for controlling objects by command and thus opens up new possibilities for research. By giving the older handicapped child access to the computer, not only do we see his initial abilities — a measure of the effect of growing up without control — but we get to study the profile of his continuing learning, a profile that may yield information of great importance not only for the handicapped child, but also for cognitive science in general. Developmental investigations beginning very early, perhaps in the handicapped child's infancy, should help us answer questions about the relationship between "remote control" manipulations and cognition. It would also be useful to compare the cognitive development stages of the handicapped child with those that Piaget and others have so meticulously documented for the normal child.

SOME CONJECTURED SOLUTIONS TO THE DILEMMA

On one hand, careful researchers and theorists are agreed that doing promotes learning, while mere watching or listening does not. On the other hand, we know people who, to the best of our knowledge, can only watch or listen and yet still learn. It seems important to explain this general agreement of scholars despite the evidence that forces us to question their theories.

Motivational Factors

The observation that physical activity fosters learning might be ascribed to motivational factors involved in hands-on experiences. The fact that children spend more time at things they enjoy is unquestionable. Some relationship between time spent and material learned might be posited, but children also love to sit and watch television. If children learn from television, then it is not their physical activity that has promoted the learning. If they do not learn from it, then motivation and the time spent are not sufficient for learning. Either way, motivation from physical activity seems like a weak explanation for observed improvements in learning. We might, while we are thinking about this, ask why a child is motivated by physically active lessons — and for that matter, why he is motivated by such a sedentary pastime as watching TV? Why do most children seem motivated by computers?

Multimodal Learning

Another characteristic of physically active lessons that might explain why they seem so very much more powerful than verbally presented lessons is this: The normal child who engages in a physical activity not only is availed of the inherent enactive representation, but also sees what he does as well. If he is not already translating one of those two modalities into symbolic representation, he is most likely receiving some semblance of a symbolic representation from his teacher — any instructions that call his particular attention to some feature or another serve to build up this verbal coding on top of visual and motoric coding.

Anyone who has taught a language lesson in which one participant of a pair describes a simple picture in words and the other draws the picture or selects it from a small set of samples knows that the skill of making translations from iconic to symbolic representations (to use Bruner's terminology) is not, in general, very well developed. We must work to create for ourselves the visual and motoric representations of verbally given information. The child who is physically active in his lesson is most likely gaining access to the subject of the lesson with all appropriate modalities. A child attending to a verbally presented lesson does not get the motoric and visual content for free. Any particular student may not need such multimodal input in order to assimilate the information, but one might suppose this "buckshot approach" is likely to supply whichever form of input the student can most easily encode and make use of. When we look at the performance of groups of children, therefore, we might well expect a statistical benefit from such teaching.

Attentionality

An even more simple-minded explanation of the superiority of action-based learning situations is that attention to the task may be heightened when motor activity is involved.

Both the multimodal learning and attentionality theories can be tested. Measures of arousal, orienting response, and attention exist. There are children whose learning appears to be hampered by multimodal presentations, and there are children who never get multimodal presentations. The deaf-blind child presumably does not get free iconic and symbolic representations along with an enactive one. Cerebral palsy and deaf-blindness are both naturally occurring situations that reduce or remove the interaction of motor learning with other forms of learning. Careful research in these areas would help to clarify the role of each of these modalities in cognitive development.

A BRIEF RESTATEMENT

There is a tremendous appeal to the old proverb

> I hear and I forget;
> I see and I remember;
> I do and I understand.

Our collective experience supports it, Piaget's meticulous observations appear to support it, Bruner's theories support it, Kephart's recommendations to teachers support it, and practicing teachers often say they support it, yet there is another body of data that we must explain. Old-fashioned "sit in your chair and face front" teaching, despite its various failings, did succeed with at least some children, and severely physically handicapped children do learn despite being prevented by their condition from having what Lowenthal considers essential experiences:

> Moving [their] whole body in various ways (jumping, running, etc.) taking things apart and putting them back together, imitating the actions of people, animals and objects.... (1978, pp. 310, 311)

I, too, believe that "objects should be provided for [the child] to touch or move as he repeats a number aloud" (Ault, 1977, p. 177). I believe this because:

Children enjoy touching and moving things, as do I, and I know of no study that says enjoyment is harmful

It seems generally wasteful to restrict the modalities through which any person would normally experience his environment

When a teacher has a child exercise the form of counting separate from the function of counting, the separation of form from function is implicitly accepted, a separation that I personally do not like

However, and most importantly, none of these reasons is a statement of educational psychology or science — the reasons are all matters of my own personal taste. For that matter, my own experience as a teacher shows that the activity approach works very well, despite confusions in the theories that attempt to explain it. However, I certainly do not believe that I have ever seen any evidence that "verbal abstractions...are not active enough...to produce learning" (Ault, 1977, p. 178). The very acquisition of language is an example of a child's learning by manipulating verbal abstractions. Certainly the child's ability to make correct use of the words "the," "of," and "gotta" is not the result of an organized curriculum of concrete activities that teach those words. Why then do we assume that the correct use of "red," "three," and "circle" cannot be achieved without such a curriculum?

What does make sense is that abnormal experiential deficits or abnormal experiential content bring about abnormal learning, but this should direct our attention to normalizing experience and not to predigesting it. We must adjust input, not by structuring it ourselves, but by providing an input source that is natural and accessible enough to allow handicapped persons to structure it themselves. Since children normally experience control, we must endeavor to provide that experience for the handicapped child as well. The computer makes an ideal servant.

Chapter 4
Deafness, Language,
and Cognitive Development

THE CHILDREN

The problems of the physically disabled child and the barriers that restrict his interaction with the world are visible, making it easy to illustrate the value that a computer can have for him. This is not so with the deaf child, whose greatest special needs result from isolation from information, something that can neither be seen nor felt. In an academic setting, this isolation (e.g., an inability to read fluently at his interest or intellectual level) keeps him dependent on others for information and contributes to a high failure rate. Academic failure comes from at least three sources:

The "natural" loss of information that deaf people experience because so much goes unheard

The focus of so much of a deaf child's education on skills (speech and speechreading) that his handicap makes difficult if not impossible for him

The English language deficit that keeps most prelingually deaf children from reading well, and that therefore greatly interferes with all academic progress in conventional settings

The added dependence makes autonomy difficult and costly. Repeated failure often destroys academic motivation, or at least the will to experiment, and generally takes a toll in the child's feelings of self-worth.

In the descriptions of Peter, Phillip, and Gordon, it is these aspects of the interaction — the motivation, experimentation, and feelings of self-worth — that are especially worthy of note. The computer is a servant rewarding the child's autonomy. (See the Appendix for detailed transcriptions from videotape, which are included to preserve as much information about Phillip and Peter's thinking, planning, and use of language as possible.)

Philip — "Correct! Fine! Easy!"

Phillip is an 11-year-old deaf boy with an additional visual handicap. His vision is adequate for normal-sized print, but only if he holds the book fairly close to his face. He is obviously bright, and is active and sociable, but his deafness and poor vision cause problems in academics.

Phillip set up a problem in which he would drive the turtle through a passageway of blocks that he built for it. His work was punctuated with enthusiastic chirps and a lot of bouncing back and forth, some of which was the result of his poor vision, which required that he get up to look at the turtle's moves closely. As he guided the turtle, he occasionally selected blocks to use as rulers to find out if the turtle was aimed in the right direction or had moved far enough. When the turtle had done what he wanted, he congratulated it. Once he even shook hands with himself! When things went wrong, Phillip occasionally would shake a fist in mock anger at the "dumb" turtle, and then correct his instructions to it. It was very clear that he knew who was in charge and he was feeling competent. His anthropomorphizing made the whole event an amusing fantasy.

These excerpts from the transcript indicate some of the personal involvement that was so obvious in watching him. Phillip's signing is shown in italics.

He watched as the newly corrected FORWARD 50 was executed, leaned slightly toward the turtle, and gave it three short, deliberate claps. His expression was a humorous combination of being genuinely pleased with himself and applauding his efforts, while teasing the turtle as if to say "Congratulations, dummy, for finally figuring out which way to go!"
Phillip rotated the turtle back toward the left, straightening it as he continued to park it. Again he applauded the turtle, but this time with a much smaller gesture and with not a trace of sarcasm — entirely a compliment to the beautiful turn the turtle had just executed at his command. He looked up at Ellen [teaching him] as he clapped. Ellen clapped a light clap, too, and walked back to the table. FORWARD. He walked up to the table himself, clapped one loud clap for the turtle, looked up at Ellen, and returned to finish the job. One more FORWARD did it. He looked up, signed a very casual one-handed *celebrate*, much like the bored "whoopie!" of someone who has just succeeded in doing something but does not want to let on that it was any work at all. His smile was the giveaway. With a little, cocky, oh-it-was-nothing shake of the head, he turned back to the console. There was nothing else to do, so he got up, removed the middle wall, and changed the problem. He signed several moves that the turtle might make, but was again thinking out loud rather than trying to communicate. No clear goal was really established this time. He pointed to the pen in the turtle, showed *up* with his thumb, returned to the seat and spelled *PU, PU, correct!* while verbalizing "pen up." He typed PU and watched the result. It was the first time that he had given that command. He was so very pleased with the result that he gave the turtle one solid clap and then shook hands with himself!
The seventh minute.   He pulled himself up straight in his chair, and, as he tossed his head slightly back, he made a gracefully florid gesture upward with an upturned palm, beckoning the pen to move up with a princely signed command! His pride was crowned as he placed his hands on his hips to show how easy it had been. What power! Movement at his command! He finished his story: *correct!, it moved up, fine, easy!* saying "pen up" as he signed *up*. He paused to think what comes next and held his mouth closed, meaning "don't tell me." He followed that with an "oh well' shoulder shrug and then some more typing. A typographical error spurred an animated "wrong" and a chirp. After shaking a fist at himself, he signed *wrong* again, this time somewhat more subdued and accompanied by a spoken "wrong." He commanded the turtle to back up, and before the command had a chance to be executed, ran over to the turtle, bent over it with his hands folded behind his

back, and smiled upon it as it followed his order. With a single triumphant
clap, he put a hand up in a policeman-like "stop" sign and hooted a pleased
"oop." Exactly seven minutes.

When a friend wandered by, near the end of the session, Phillip beck-
oned him over, grabbed his hand, and used the friend's fingers to type
instructions to the turtle. How else would you introduce a friend to the
turtle?

Peter — "Smart!"

Peter is 12 years old and has only begun to sign within the last year, with no
prior evidence of any shared language. He has had a history of many unsuc-
cessful foster placements, all terminated because of severe and unmanageable
behavior problems. When he was accepted at his current residential treatment center, his record included a misdiagnosis of autism. Long before he
was taught a sharable language, he was apparently picking up information
that we tend to think of as being transmitted only through linguistic means.
He is, for example, able to reminisce about some of his experiences in early
foster placements, identifying places and dates accurately. It is not known
how Peter gained this information.

Like Phillip, Peter set himself tasks with the turtle, and, as soon as
one was finished, set up another. He was constantly asking questions and
attended carefully to the answers, following up the question if he did not
fully understand the answer. Although he was less playful than Phillip, especially at first, he was not at all timid about experimenting. His demeanor, the questions that he asked, and the way that he asked them all
suggested an almost scholarly interest in understanding this new machine.
Unlike Phillip, whose excitement seemed to come from the control that he
exercised and the playful aspects of driving this turtle robot through his
own obstacle course, Peter was excited primarily by discovering how this
gadget worked. At first, when he did not fully comprehend that the command that told the turtle to move forward also told it how far to move, he
was concerned with how to stop the turtle after having told it to go.
Rather late in his first session with the turtle, he showed clearly how pleased with himself he was. He effectively caught Ellen's attention and signed
Smart!.

Peter and Phillip signed to themselves as they were working. Both
evaluated their work, considered themselves smart, and felt considerable
pride. Both recognized and corrected errors and planned and set up new
challenges for themselves. Both worked with real energy and animation.

Gordon

Gordon was 6 years old when he began working with the CARIS program
(Geoffrion and Bergeron, 1978). During the first session, CARIS pre-

sented a list of eight nouns, including GIRL, BOY, HOUSE, TURTLE, BIRD, and DOG, from which Gordon could choose one by pointing to it with a special pointer. When he selected a noun, the list would disappear and a large line drawing (captioned with the noun at the bottom of the screen) would appear, illustrating his chosen word. A second or so later, another list would appear that contained verbs, such as WALKS, RUNS, SHRINKS, GROWS, JUMPS, and FLIES. Selecting a verb would then animate the cartoon. Again the cartoon was captioned below with the two-word sentence.

Gordon was just beginning to read and knew none of the words on the CARIS lists before he started. The following excerpted transcription from videotape summarizes Gordon's first 4 minutes with CARIS (Geoffrion, 1977).

He picked GIRL JUMPS. After the animation was finished, he traced the girl's trajectory on the screen with his two fingers, as if signing the word JUMP on the TV screen. He watched until the girl disappeared from the screen. Tapping his teacher's arm to get her attention, he signed the action on the screen again, clearly describing what he had just seen. His teacher said "She jumped?" and the two of them signed *jump* together.

The second time he ran down the list, he was clearly searching for something in particular. He picked BOY. As soon as the picture appeared, he turned to his teacher and signed *again!* and scanned the list for JUMPS. As before, he repeated the jump sign on the screen after the animation was finished. The next time he picked TURTLE RUNS, selecting the words much less deliberately than before. After watching the animation, he pointed to the words at the bottom of the screen and looked to his teacher who signed them to him. For his next animation, he again picked turtle, but changed the verb to JUMPS. After selecting TURTLE the third time, he signed *again* and chose WALKS. Gordon followed the turtle's slow walk across the screen with his finger. He experimented with a few different nouns and verbs and then picked GIRL. He pointed to a verb and looked to his teacher. She said (but did not sign) "walks"? He pointed to another verb and queried again. This time it was a verb he had not used before. She began to sign *flies,* but caught herself before she said it out loud. Shrugging her shoulders, she signed and said "try." She muttered to herself "Gerry, don't tell him!" and then repeated out loud and with sign, "try, try it!" He did, and he enjoyed the new animation. Her expression showed pleasant surprise. The next time he went directly back to TURTLE. As had occasionally happened earlier, the pointer did not work the first time and so he had to touch the pointer again to TURTLE, this time with more deliberate attention. It was very clear that he wanted that particular word and no other. When it got his turtle and verb list, he scanned it briefly and, apparently remembering the effect, pointed directly to FLIES. After several more trials, mostly using JUMPS, he discovered the noun BIRD, one he had not used before. He looked at the picture, signed *bird* and then immediately scanned the verb list for FLIES.

Periodically throughout this session, Gordon's teacher commented on how quickly Gordon was mastering this sight vocabulary. Gordon was recognized as a bright child, but the usual history of teaching new words, particularly verbs, to Gordon and his classmates suggested that 16 words in a 15-minute session was extremely fast. His teacher's notes (Foss, 1977, personal communication) included the following:

> Just fantastic — smiling a lot — turns to me, points and smiles — picks a specific word regardless of random order [presentation of lists] — signs after he chooses word, but before picture appears — follows action of a verb with finger — Very exuberant on walk back — acts out verbs "skip" and "hop"

This kind of system might be used with much younger children, as well. Some of Geoffrion's experiments with early prototypes of CARIS were done with a 4-year-old.

THE EDUCATIONAL HANDICAP OF DEAFNESS

The vast majority of people who become deaf before the age of 3 do not acquire the same fluency in English as their hearing peers. Even the commonly mentioned fifth-grade reading level (beyond which more than half of these people presumably never develop their reading skills) is probably a misleadingly high assessment of the ability of the prelingually deaf adult to gain information through reading (Brill, 1974). Of course, this seriously restricts normal interaction with the rest of the business, academic, and social world. Not only is the deaf person's access to public information reduced by his inability to make effective use of television (or any use of radio), but even newspapers are poor sources of information for the person whose understanding of written English is limited.

Face-to-face communication, at least with most other deaf adults, is not the issue here. Internally, a deaf society gets along well without speech and hearing, and direct interpersonal communication in American Sign Language does not require a knowledge of English. Access to public information channels, such as the news media, legal documents, job applications, government publications, and books, however, does require such knowledge.

The most profound *educational* handicap of the deaf person would have to be his difficulties with written English. The deaf person's difficulties with reading and writing English are no more than reflections of a lack of knowledge of the language. Hearing children acquire the language naturally and grow up with the experience of using their language to control others long before they encounter school lessons. In contrast, prelingually deaf children typically get most or all of their English (and frequently their first systematic sign language) in school, where the predominant role of language is responding, rather than initiating or controlling. Although their English is developed as a tool, it is not really theirs to use. Rather, it is a means for others to control them. Unless English is of service to these children, their spontaneous use of it will be minimal. There is good reason to believe that language simply cannot develop in the absence of communicative purpose.

Before we can feel responsible about putting effort into developing techniques for teaching fluent Standard English (SE) to a prelingually deaf person, we must convince ourselves that there is no theoretical reason why this should be impossible. There are three arguments that contain sufficiently important questions about the learning of written English to be worth mentioning here, yet they ultimately fail to explain the lack of success educators have had in teaching written English to deaf students.

Perhaps a communication system cannot be learned well if its transmission rate falls outside of the normal range for natural languages. Neither writing nor sign systems that attempt to give a morpheme-by-morpheme manual presentation of SE can match the information transmission rate of speech or American Sign Language (ASL).

Perhaps hearing is the only modality by which a child can get the critical minimum of English input to learn the language in any form.

Perhaps the best modality for learning a language is that modality within which the language developed. English developed as a spoken language. Face-to-face conversation makes such extensive use of pause, tone of voice, facial expression, and gesture that committing merely the spoken words to print renders most conversations almost unintelligible. Punctuation, underlining, page format, and syntactic and stylistic constraints of written English all attempt to convey some of the information that would have been available if the words had been spoken. Written English is certainly different from spoken English; perhaps it is less learnable.

As has been suggested, if any of these explanations were correct, then teaching English to a deaf child would be a hopeless cause. Fortunately, these explanations are inadequate. We certainly know of many situations in which foreign languages have been taught (and learned well!) only in their written forms. When a student studies Latin from a text, for instance, he suffers both the slowness and the lack of input that the deaf child suffers in studying English.[10] Yet these limitations do not necessarily stop him from attaining excellence in the language. As for the stylistic constraints, I do not know of any reason why written English is any less "natural" a language than spoken English.

The use of sign language is often invoked as an explanation of the deaf child's difficulties with English. Interference between two languages is quite small when compared with the English problems usually experienced by the deaf person, and thus it cannot fully explain these problems. The fact that sign would have a chance to interfere with English at all might be attributed to the natural preference, even in oral schools, that many deaf children feel for sign because it is such an effective communication medium. Rather than banning sign — a solution chosen in some schools — it seems more valuable to introduce a highly motivating set of activities in which written English is the most effective medium.

Critical period arguments remain discouraging, but it is hard to make a thoroughly convincing case that the deaf child's difficulties with English are due more to the existence of a critical period than to his continuing and overwhelming lack of communicative experience with English, even after he has begun to receive deliberate instruction.

ISSUES IN DEAF EDUCATION

The controversies surrounding the education of deaf children might well be the most bitter I have ever seen, with each side accusing the other of ignoring or deliberately hiding the facts and resorting to scare tactics and political invective to coerce parents into joining their crusade. The result is a hodgepodge of claims and counterclaims that maintain not even a pretense at impartiality. It was possible for a speaker at the National Convention of the Alexander Graham Bell Association to swear, to be loudly applauded, and to get the whole event published (for example, Ling in Scherer et al. 1972, p. 554). Edwin Martin chaired a panel presentation on the controversy, and despite his plea for moderation in what he called the "emotional and mindless debate that drags on merely for the sake of battle" (p. 528), the battle raged on. Papers headlined their inflammatory contents with equally inflammatory titles: "Mind Over Mouth: A Ra-

---

[10]I do not mean to dismiss lightly the difficulties of learning English as a first systematic shared language at age 6 by comparing them glibly to the task of learning Latin after 10 or more years of fluency in a first language. The lack of an early, fluent first language is not at issue here. The deaf infant could be provided with fluent ASL were we to decide that the benefits were worth the difficulties. Here I am simply suggesting that Written English is, in principle, learnable in the absence of spoken use.

tionale for Total Communication" (Vernon, 1972) and "'Total Communication' — Fraud or Reality?'' (Drumm, 1972).

It is not my purpose to join the fight in this present piece of writing, but there are three important issues that I wish to address and for which I must present some background. I have frequently become quite distressed with the fact that what seem to me to be the real issues in deaf education (the very same issues as in any education) have frequently been submerged under mythology, occasionally in the guise of "science." To help the reader focus on the real issues, a task I find difficult at times when reading political rhetoric, I state the issues here:

We are interested in finding a modality through which the deaf child can exercise and develop his mind without being any more handicapped at that exercise than is a normal child.

We are interested in learning more about the deaf child's thinking, particularly as it may elucidate the nature of the relationship between thinking and language and as it may provide us with practical methods for improving the education of deaf people.

We are interested in ferreting out and debugging the myths that conceal the issues.

It is my contention that the computer, used by the deaf child as his own tool, and not as his teacher's, provides a powerful and nondiscriminatory modality for cognitive exploration. Considerable information about the thinking of the child also may be obtained by thoughtful observations of the child's experiments and projects.

THE SALVOS IN THE HUNDRED-YEARS' WAR

Vernon (1972) presents six arguments favoring total communication:

1. Most deaf adults were educated orally, and yet the "overwhelming majority," both as individuals and in organizations such as the National Association of the Deaf, oppose oralism.
2. The articulation of two-thirds of English phonemes is either invisible or visually indistinguishable from that of other phonemes. With a good command of English, one can use discoursive, contextual, syntactic and semantic constraints to help resolve some of the ambiguities. As a result, the best speechreaders are hearing people, *not* deaf. Even they can read only about 25% of what is said in normal speech while the average deaf child, lacking facility with English, gets only about 5%. Vernon regards having to *learn* English in this way as "ridiculous" and "cruel." (See also Farwell, 1976.)

3. Vernon asserts that advocates of auralism are "blur[ing] the distinction between the reality and the wishes and fantasies surrounding this reality" (p. 532). He asserts that those children in the U.S. with hearing losses of 85 dB or greater who are now in programs for the "hearing impaired" (more than 50% of the total enrollment) will not be able to learn language through the use of amplification, no matter how intense. Using *hearing impairment* or another "soft" term, rather than using *deafness,* "which objectively describes the problem," is ultimately harsh and cruel.

4. With total communication in home and school, "the deaf child sees language continually and learns it incidentally as hearing children do" (p. 532).

5. Vernon summarizes numerous studies documenting "the 100-year failure of oral education" and indicates that total communication "improves academic performance to the point of doubling reading gains" (p. 534) without adversely affecting the acquisition of speech or speechreading skills.

6. He concludes with a psychological argument:

> The gross deprivation of the opportunity to communicate openly with one's parents and family which the ambiguity of oralism/auralism entails is irreversibly crippling psychologically. It denies deaf children the basic information and civilized interaction necessary for normal human development. (p. 536)

Vernon views the disregard of the repeated arguments and numerous studies favoring total communication as a form of denial, psychologically motivated by an unwillingness to accept the reality of deafness (Vernon, 1967, 1968, 1969, 1970, 1971, 1972; Vernon and Koh, 1970, 1971; Mindel and Vernon, 1971). The opposition charges that Vernon has censored, distorted, and ignored the data, used poor and unreliable sources, misrepresented and/or misunderstood oralism/auralism, and been repetitive and extremist (DiCarlo, 1972; Ling in Scherer et al., 1972).

The briefest statement of position that I think does justice to the views of the total communicationists is that they believe that a fully fluent communication system should be available as early and as effortlessly for deaf children as it is for hearing children. There is evidence that this approach leads to cognitive, linguistic, social, and emotional gains for the child without jeopardizing and likely aiding his acquisition of more conventional communication forms, such as English reading and writing, speech, and speechreading.

Oralist/auralists, on the other hand, feel that the total communicationists defeat the deaf by expecting less than is attainable and locking them into a permanently handicapped existence. They feel that sign language interferes with the acquisition of speech and speechreading skills, and because its rules are not like English, it is one of the significant causes of "deaf English." Historically, oralism did not have the technology available to include today's aural approaches as well, but the oral/aural philosophy is now augmented by their belief (illustrated by numerous case studies) that

> A child's hearing loss can be functionally changed! A deaf child can live his life with a use of hearing.... It no longer remains true that deaf children must learn visually or even depend upon lipreading for the majority of their language input. (Conner, 1972, pp. 523–524)

Modern technology has significantly improved the power and compactness of hearing aids. Developments are now being made that will allow these aids to be personally tailored to the particular hearing loss of each user (Elliot, 1978). The oralist/auralists state that early aural training can habilitate even the most marginal hearing and lead it to usefulness rather than atrophy. Furthermore, microelectronics has finally made practical a rather old idea of providing a deaf person with a "wearable eyeglass speechreading aid" (Upton, 1968) that should vastly reduce the difficulty of speechreading and make it a quite practical, nearly fluent means of communication for many deaf persons. Thus, the oralist/auralist dream of giving deaf children functional use of hearing, fluent speechreading, and understandable speech is receiving support from technological advances. In addition to claiming this strength, the oralists claim the better morality. In Conner's (1972) words:

> We are not debating a method for classrooms; we are deciding...whether a handicapped child shall be a member of a deaf subculture or a hearing impaired person whose philosophy and life objectives are as wide as those of the rest of the human race. (pp. 523–524)

How do we compare these two schools of thought, which potentially dictate different policies for computer-aided instruction? In 1972, Vernon said that no professionally published research that made comparisons between oralism and total communication concluded by supporting oralism. I have seen none since. The research that does support oralism is not comparitive, but rather evaluates the success that one or another particular school had has with the oral method. A recent example of this orientation in research is Lane's (1976) paper "The Profoundly Deaf: Has Oral Education Succeeded?"

The issues are further confused by such statements as "The single major need for any deaf child is for a consistent overwhelming quantity of straight language input and output" (Conner, 1967, p. 265).

In the words of John Willis (personal communication, psychoeducational specialist, the Communication and Learning Group, Inc., Durham N.H.), "I would have put my money on food and air." The single major need for *anybody* is to be able to lead an enjoyable and estimable life. This is not a scientific statement, but a statement of value, and one I do not imagine Conner would have disavowed. What Conner must have meant was that it was his *theory* that such an estimable and enjoyable life would be best facilitated by having the skills that, according to another *theory* of his, "a consistent overwhelming quantity of straight language input and output" would bring about. The value statement is, of course, not scientifically testable, but the theoretical statements (recast somewhat more precisely than I have cast them here) are. It is precisely because theory, value, wish, and prediction are so mixed in Conner's (1967) writing that his statements are of little scientific worth. "The aim for every deaf child is to initiate and establish habitual speechreading, understandably articulated speech, and a receptive and expressive vocabulary of hundreds of words and verbal concepts by the fifth birthday" (p. 266). Whatever the difference between "words" and "verbal concepts" was intended to be, "hundreds...by the fifth birthday" is a pathetically small goal. This vocabulary is like that of the normal 2-and-one-half-year-old, not the normal 5-year-old, who has upward of 2,000 words (Moskowitz, 1978, citing Madorah E. Smith). It is now the straight-English people, the oralist/auralists, who appear to be expecting less than is attainable.

That Conner (1967) confuses scientific with political issues is perhaps most clearly demonstrated by the next statement, a prescription that suggests nothing researched or researchable and that seems to have been made in reaction to the publication of Furth's *Thinking Without Language* (1966), an investigation into the cognitive development of the deaf child. "Whether the deaf child ever did or can 'think without language' is a useless question to debate, for the deaf child must think with language like every other human being" (Conner, 1967, p. 266). I had not realized that the nature of human thought had been clarified so completely.

LANGUAGE AND THINKING

Unlike the thinking of the cerebral palsied child, the thinking of the deaf child has been the subject of considerable study. Some of this study has suffered from the kinds of misconceptions that run rampant through the oral-manual controversy. However, the relationship between language and thought, for the most part, is a research issue rather than a service issue. Perhaps the explanation of the fact that investigations in this area are not as muddy as investigations of teaching practices is that people find it easier to test and reject a research hypothesis than to test and reject a career.

Although the relationship of thinking and language has received a lot of research, some of it, especially as it is done with deaf children, is contaminated by cultural myth uninformed by scientific studies.

The notions that thinking is a kind of internalized language and that it depends fully for its existence on the development of language seems to be a part of our cultural inheritance. "Dumb" means both speechless and witless. People who cannot speak *our* language seem "dumb" to us, and the history, even recent history, of misdiagnosis of the intelligence of non-English speaking youngsters is shameful. Schools have designed programs around the myth that thinking requires words. Although the practice of teaching Classical Greek to improve children's analytic minds has nearly vanished, the influences of that kind of thinking can still be seen. I still hear that argument about Latin occasionally. Mathematics, a more grammatically restricted language than Greek or Latin, but just as much a language, is often justified because it teaches a student how to think. Quite commonly, when people first find out that I work with deaf children, I am asked how they think if they can't speak! Do they *see* the words? Do they think (dream) in sign language? Although these questions may seem naive to the developmental psychologist or the psycholinguist, they are quite common among other well-educated professionals.

The Language

The deaf child is a natural subject for research on the relationship of language to thinking, provided that some definitions are kept in order. Not having speech and not having English are different. Not having English and not having a sharable language are different. Finally, not having a *shared* language and not having *any* language are different. The linguistic experience of deaf children, particularly with respect to the last two points, needs some clarification.

Not having English does not mean not having any sharable language. Only about 10% of prelingually deaf children have deaf parents, but the vast majority of that 10% are brought up on American Sign Language (ASL), the language of their parents. Their acquisition of sign language closely parallels the hearing child's development of English in both pattern and schedule except for the possibility that the very first signs may appear somewhat earlier than the very first words. ASL is not sharable with the vast majority of Americans (although of the non-English languages, only Spanish and Italian are used by more Americans!), but during the first few years of life, children usually do not involve themselves with the vast majority of Americans anyway. ASL is not English-on-the-hands, but it is a true language, fully as productive, as precise, as powerful at conveying complex and abstract ideas, and as capable of poetry and metaphor as any other language, e.g., English (Wilbur, 1976). Yet, non-linguists who work with the deaf continue to present linguistically naive views of sign language.

> Signing has a great deal of limitations. There are just between two and three thousand words in the lexicon and, if you look at normal language, this appears to be little. University entrants, for example, have 75,000 words according to Oldfield. There's a fantastic discrepancy between the number of units available. (Ling, in Scherer et al., 1972, p. 553)

Only because that particular misconception is so popular do I feel the need of addressing it directly. Counting the words in one spoken language, let alone making comparisons of the sizes of two different lexicons is not an endeavor that linguists take at all seriously. It is possible to number the words people use in day-to-day conversations, although even then there are some nontrivial decisions to be made about what to consider distinct words (e.g., how many different words are in the set containing speak, speaks, speech, speaker, spoken [as in spoken English], and speaking [as in English-speaking]?). Still, since Ling claims to be comparing the *total lexicon* of ASL to the *usable vocabulary* of certain English speakers, one might think that, even allowing for a very large margin of error, the two figures do show a "fantastic discrepancy." Ling's 2,000 to 3,000 words is an often quoted figure based unthinkingly on the sizes of the available sign language *dictionaries*. For one thing, these dictionaries were generally severely limited in scope for purely financial reasons. Second, these dictionaries are pioneer efforts by very small numbers of people — never over a handful centrally involved — and have a history extending back barely over a decade. Finally, the problems of counting lexical entries in ASL is compounded by the fact that there is not yet a particularly well-defined and agreed upon principle for doing it (Stokoe, Casterline, and Croneberg, 1976).

What about the 90% of deaf children whose parents are hearing and do not know sign language? Due to the still predominant late diagnosis of deafness and the tendency for hearing parents not to learn the language most easily acquirable by their deaf infants, most of these children do not have a fluent and sharable language for several years, some not until they are 5 or 6 years of age. (Recall Conner's goal that the deaf child have "hundreds of words... by the fifth birthday.") The key word here is *sharable*. What coding schemes various deaf children use for their symbolic handling of the world is not known. (There seems no a priori reason to assume that different deaf children would code their experiences the same way.) Whether these schemes are "linguistic" is, at the least, a terribly premature question. It is clear that deaf children have what Ricks and Wing (1976) call "inner language." It therefore seems rash, if only because one is left somewhat free to decide what precisely is meant, to make a statement that "Research... on deaf children has shown that cognitive growth can progress surprisingly well in human beings who have little or no command of any sort of linguistic system" (Flavell, 1977, p. 237). We have Peter's reminiscences of his "prelinguistic years" to contend with!

The Thinking

Research on the cognitive behavior of deaf children has shown their achievements to be essentially the same as that of hearing children in all tasks that do not require linguistic mediation. This result has been used by Furth (1966, 1973) and others to make arguments such as Flavell's.

Although research shows that deaf children progress beautifully through all of Piaget's stages to arrive successfully at formal operations as a deaf adult, they pass through each of these stages somewhat later than hearing children (Furth, 1966; Best and Roberts, 1975). Deaf children and adults are noted to be less able to discover a pattern than their hearing peers, but equally able to comprehend and use the pattern once they have discovered it or have had it shown to them. This and other evidence is sometimes explained as rigidity in their thinking. "Their inability or slowness in shifting from one principle or viewpoint to another has frequently been noted" (Furth, 1966). Furth (1966) convincingly argues that these differences, although real, have nothing to do with linguistic deficits.

> Although deaf children are somewhat late in giving mature responses to Piaget's task, the principal point to keep in mind is that no deaf adult believes that the amount of liquid changes with changing containers or that there are more inhabitants of New Jersey than there are Americans. If the deaf appear rigid in a certain sense and adhere to a given viewpoint, is it because they have no understanding of the possible or that they have been socially trained to stay in the position they have found secure? If they fail to reason, is it because they cannot reason or because they are not motivated to reason?
>
> As I observed deaf people, both in natural and experimental situations, I became increasingly convinced that the second alternative of each of the foregoing questions is more reasonable and scientifically justifiable. Deaf people

behave as they do...as a result of their social environment. This includes their early homes, their schooling, the deaf community within the hearing community, each with its social attitudes, stereotypes and other environmental factors. (pp. 150–151)

Two common experiences of the deaf child stand out as particularly likely causes of the intellectual conservatism so often noted. That the deaf child tends not to discover patterns might be a function of the overwhelming emphasis that is made on copying, drilling, and practicing. If what Vernon calls the ambiguity of oral/aural communication could provide an opportunity for "creative language processing," it might actually be a genuine blessing to the deaf child. In fact, such is not the case. The virtues of ambiguity for discovery tasks are lost when the stakes for being correct are so high. Communication is too important. One must understand correctly, not imaginatively!

Unfortunately, this emphasis on drill and practice transcends the oral-manual controversy. It has been my experience that all schools — even those using total communication — very heavily stress watching, copying, and being correct — especially in English, where patterns, if not explicitly stated somewhere in rule form, are drilled for perfection, and rules are taught as rules. This is particularly true of computer-aided instruction, where drill and practice have been the predominant model all along. This approach must be deemed categorically wrong for deaf children.

Young, language-learning deaf children, like language-learning hearing children, undoubtedly need to "construct their initial grammars on the basis of the short, simple, grammatical sentences that are addressed to them in the first year or two they speak" (Moskowitz, 1978, p. 94b). However, also like hearing children, deaf children need to construct their own model of language from the linguistic input that they receive. "There is no evidence at all to suggest that a deaf child is a less capable linguistic 'agent' than a hearing child" (Brennan, 1975, p. 464). Moskowitz (1978) has stated that

Since each child's utterances at a particular stage are from her own point of view grammatically correct, it is not surprising that children are fairly impervious to the correction of their language by adults, indeed to any attempts to teach them language.... Courtney B. Cazden of Harvard University found that children benefit less from frequent adult correction of their errors than from true conversational interaction. Indeed, correcting errors can interrupt that interaction, which is, after all, the function of language. (pp. 94b, 94d)

Since "there is some evidence to suggest that by denying the child the opportunity to construct his own language, we ensure that he will never fully master any language system" (Brennan, 1975, p. 464), the deaf child's education ought to include as much interactive language in use as possible. Brennan urges us to consider the child as an active agent in the acquisition process, saying that "the purely imitative model of language acquisition... fails ultimately because it views the child as passively assimilating rather than actively operating upon, linguistic data" (p. 464). Brennan further says, "The child is active not only in the construction of his language system but also in making that system work for him" (p. 464).

We must conclude that if computers are to be helpful to the deaf child's learning of English, we will have to provide interactive English-in-use, rather than grammar lessons, that is, opportunities for the deaf child to use and play with his own language, not merely to expose it and have it altered.

Chapter 5
Autism, Perception,
and Cognitive Development

Most of this chapter focuses on research issues specific to autism. The examples of children working with computers, however, include a mixture of children, not all of whom are or were ever thought to be autistic. Although the clinical pictures of these children are not much the same — they are very much not a coherent group — they all illustrate some of the educational considerations that become important when the limiting factor in a child's use of a computer is not apparently sensory or motor.

COGNITIVELY HANDICAPPED CHILDREN

The cognitive capacity of the children I have described so far was, in some cases, questioned by diagnosticians, but I have consistently indicated my own reservations about these diagnoses and have stressed the brightness of the children. By contrast, I am willing to accept the judgment that all five children described in this chapter have serious cognitive handicaps. This, of course, raises another issue. Whatever "cognitively handicapped" should turn out to mean — and this will come up a bit later — you should probably view my assessment that these children are cognitively handicapped with the same suspicion that I expressed about the diagnoses made by others.

Nancy, Joey, Kevin, and Thomas had been at some time considered autistic, although for Nancy that diagnosis is now disputed. Annette was never thought to be autistic. Her evaluation contains uncertainties and conflicting information. She is classified as mentally retarded with severe language and perceptual disabilities.

Nancy — "Aren't you happy at me!"

Nancy is 5 years old. Her original diagnoses include early childhood autism. Although that diagnosis is now in question, her behavior and communication are quite clearly very disturbed. At times she appears lost in a world of her own and she sometimes talks to objects or people in that world. When she speaks, her wording is often idiosyncratic and her inflection stereotyped. When she entered the unfamiliar surroundings of our laboratory, she was clutching onto her teacher with her left hand and pinching her eyes shut with her right.

I showed Nancy the TV-turtle. Since Nancy is a very young child and not yet able to read, I thought she would do best with the "slot-machine" as an input device. Each instruction to the turtle is shown as an ideographic symbol on a plastic card that she could insert in a slot in the machine (see Figure 3). Once she has assembled a sequence of such cards, she can run the sequence by pressing a button. She played with this for a few minutes but showed no particular interest in it. With a felt tip pen, I drew

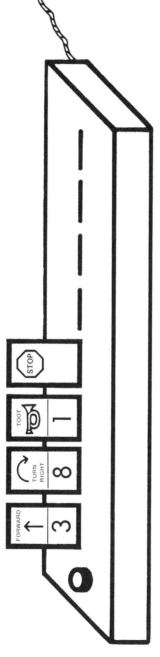

Figure 3.   The slot machine with some cards in it. The cards tell the turtle to go forward 3 steps, turn right 120°, toot once, and stop.

a simple house on the TV screen, to suggest something she might like to draw. Apparently, it suggested the use of the pen only, and so she drew her own symbols on the screen, the cards, the turtle, the table, and, once, on the terminal.

Her problem appeared to be a lack of concreteness. Drawing with a pen did something. Placing cards in a rack had no interesting effect. Pressing the button caused something to happen, but exactly what happened depended on a card sequence that was too remote in time and too unfamiliar a concept to relate to the visible effect. Finally, TV-screen drawings are a bit intangible anyway.

Conjecturing that the whole process was too distant and symbolic for her at that time, I showed her the floor turtle and placed a teletype on the floor right next to the turtle so that she and the turtle could live in the same world. To control the turtle, all she had to do was press F for forward, R for right turn, L for left turn, T for toot, etc. Although only about half a dozen keys had any effect at all, she knew her letters well, so I naively assumed there was no need to label the special keys.

She was clearly interested this time, but had difficulty keeping track of which keys produced an effect, so I stuck labels on each of the special keys. Each sticker showed only the same letter as the key it covered, but the white sticker with a red letter on it was enough to draw Nancy's attention away from the other keys. She still played with other buttons, but now appeared to do so rather deliberately. She would press F several times, watching the turtle move forward, and then would press (unlabeled and functionless) M once or twice, again looking closely at the turtle to see what would happen.

After a period of active and very clearly interested play (and some enthusiastic comments), she made a label for the M button just like the labels I had made for the other special keys. Again, she played with the various labeled buttons, including her newly labeled M button. Her making the label was described by one onlooker as a clear example of off-task repetitive behavior, but it seemed clear that she was performing an experiment. Her attempt to give M a function provided her with a great deal of information that my previous explanations had failed to convey — she stopped most of her playing with the unlabeled buttons and restricted her activities to the buttons she knew had an effect. It was also clear to her that she could cause actions that she liked by pressing the right buttons. As she gave the turtle commands to come and go and toot, I narrated the imaginary script — "You are making that turtle come to you." She directed the turtle to knock over a tower of small wooden blocks, to come to her, to run away from her, and even to talk (toot) to her at her command.

(The descriptions of the turtle's behavior, that is, "running away" or "talking" were usually initiated by me, but she seemed to enjoy my chatter and occasionally picked up on it herself.) She was communicating her own ideas to that turtle and she could see consistent and clear responses to her communications. Her interest and involvement were easily apparent to me and her teachers, and she became more active and was more in control, both of herself and of the turtle, than she had been earlier. She also said, several times, "I'm so happy at that turtle. That turtle listens to me. Aren't you happy at me!"

Joey — "Down!"

> Joey is 12 years old. He is diagnosed as autistic and "probably deaf." It is reported that he has never spoken, but he makes certain sounds repetitively at times. He does not respond to sudden loud sounds, but then neither does he respond to cuts, scrapes, and bruises, even ones than can be assumed to be fairly painful. He does not have the common autistic hand or face mannerisms, nor does he "look through" people as autistic children are famous for, but he does tend to ignore personal contact and withdraw from others. Some people working with him guess him to be bright, although nobody is in a position to say how bright.

When I worked with Joey, I occasionally signed to him despite the lack of any evidence that he understood sign language or was even watching me. I was also constantly narrating everything that I was thinking, partly for the benefit of his teacher, who was sitting nearby, but mostly to help make our videotaped documentation a little more intelligible than it would have been without a soundtrack.

We began working with the floor turtle. Joey had pushed the keys on the terminal for a short while, long enough to see that the turtle could be controlled that way, and then stretched out on the floor near the turtle, leaving me at the teletype and resting his feet by my knees. His interactions with the turtle were now physical and direct. He made it draw by pushing it around with his hands.

When the pen caught on something and fell out, he carefully turned the turtle upside down and studied the inside. During this time he did not push the turtle around, but tried repeatedly to get the pen back into its clamp, presumably so that he could continue to draw. Once he succeeded in getting it to stay in for a few seconds and then he immediately began pushing the turtle. When the pen fell out again, he stopped pushing and tried to reset the pen. It is difficult to insert it securely, but after several minutes of trying, he managed to get it to stay. Unfortunately, it was too high in its clamp so it was not in contact with the floor when Joey turned the turtle right side up. This problem was very apparent to Joey, and he did not push the turtle. For a moment he seemed to have given up, but after a pause he tried again to adjust the pen. It was clear what his intentions were and that he was willing to spend time and effort to realize them.

It took him almost 10 minutes of careful, repeated, and mostly unrewarded effort before I offered to help. He held the turtle for me while I adjusted the pen. When the pen was finally in, Joey began pushing the turtle in circles. I said, "I wonder what happens if I pick the pen up" and, from the keyboard, I withdrew the pen from the floor. Joey seemed not to notice at first, and I commented for the videotape, "He didn't notice, he didn't notice." However, without acknowledging me at all, Joey stopped pushing the turtle and said "Down!", repeating the word several times until I made the pen go down. He did not resume pushing the turtle until I got the pen back down, at which time he because quiet for a moment and then spoke again. The words were muddier this time, but there was no question but that he had said "Thank you." Joey spoke his first words on videotape and then went silently back to pushing the turtle.

It is particularly distressing that this effort could not be followed up, because what seems most impressive in this example is the possibility that the turtle might serve as a useful intermediary between Joey and a therapist or teacher. Joey can relate to that machine, and it is a relationship that can be shared with another person, as happened in this example. It is also a relationship that can change and grow with Joey, since the computer's use and behavior can be determined entirely by Joey and his teacher.

Kevin — What is Perseveration?

Kevin is 11 years old. He is diagnosed as autistic. He is clearly quite bright, and his arithmetic and spatial perception are both excellent, as is his reading. Although his speech is often communicative, it is unmistakably the stereotyped and formal speech so often noted in autistic adolescents. It is not always possible to make Kevin "hear" what has been said to him. His behavior shows the rigidity and perseveration characteristic of autism, and his attention span is described as short.

The activity we began with was an aim-the-arrow game on a TV screen. There was a small bull's-eye in the center of the screen, and somewhere on the screen an arrow pointed in some random direction (see Figure 4).

Kevin could aim the arrow right or left to face the target by giving commands, such as LEFT 165 or RIGHT 11, indicating in which direction and by how many degrees the arrow was to be re-aimed. He could also at any time shoot the arrow in the direction it was facing by typing SHOOT

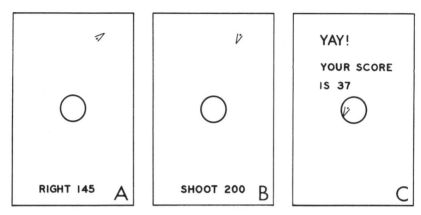

Figure 4.   The aim-the-arrow game. A: The initial setup. Kevin decides to turn the arrow right 145°. B: After aiming, Kevin decides to shoot a distance of 200°. C: He scores.

followed by a number specifiying the distance the arrow was to travel before stopping. Distances were given in hundredths of an inch, so SHOOT 155 sent the arrow 1.55 inches forward. If Kevin's arrow did not land inside the target circle (if he overshot, undershot, or otherwise missed), the arrow would stay where it "fell" for a few seconds and then be moved to a new randomly selected place. If it did hit the target, a bell would ring and Kevin would get a point added to his score.

Kevin had never studied geometry before, and did not know the measures of any angles. When he gave turning instructions to the arrow, he perseverated on large numbers that ended with 5; 165 and 155 were his favorites. In fact, repetitive use of those numbers did eventually aim the arrow correctly and he was willing to repeat the commands many times.

Whether he had an active strategy here or not was very hard to tell. Two right turns of 165° are equivalent in their effect to a left turn of 30°. A right turn of 165° followed by a left turn of 155° had the net effect of turning the arrow right 10°. There is no reason to suppose Kevin was working this out in his head, although he certainly had adequate computational abilities to do so. For one thing, he presumably did not know the number of degrees around a point so he could not use the sum-of-angles strategy. Furthermore, it would be hard to explain his generating a RIGHT 10 by such devious means as taking the difference between two angles if he actually knew what he was trying for all along.

Yet to dismiss his behavior because of its perseverative qualities is to miss a great deal of it. For one thing, when the arrow was well aimed,

Kevin spontaneously stopped turning and typed SHOOT, but this was not the only way that he showed that his perseverative behavior was quite mindful of a goal. On occasion his teacher and I would show him special angles to try, like 45°, 90°, and 180°. He tried some of them but for a long time he would return to 165° or some other favorite angle. The only time that he would consistently use an angle that was not in the mid-hundreds and ending with 5 was when the aim was very close but not quite on target. He could then be convinced (but never at other times) to try a small number like 11 (his age).

His strategy for shooting was quite different from his behavior in aiming. Kevin could aim and re-aim as much as he liked, but once he shot the arrow, he had no more chances to improve the shot. Therefore, a stereotyped use of special numbers was inappropriate for estimates of distance. He began using a ruler that we made to measure the distance to shoot the arrow rather than guessing the distances all the time, and his verbalized guesses soon became quite accurate. He became more and more deliberate in his use of angle as well as in his distance judgment, and he built up a considerable score playing with genuine enthusiasm for approximately an hour and a quarter.

The common interpretation of perseveration as being "stuck" in a response mode seems far less appropriate to describe Kevin's behavior than the assumption that his perseveration was a reasonable activity to engage in while he could think of nothing obviously better to do. Angle measure is rather mysterious; after all, instantaneously performed, RIGHT 300 looks like a left turn and RIGHT 9000 does nothing! Besides, his perseverative strategies worked. Linear measurement is far more transparent, and when he could see and understand the alternatives, he chose them.

Thomas — A Chance To Do It Right

Thomas is nine years old and autistic. He attends a special class along with six other autistic or autistic-like children. His teacher (Marshall, personal communication, Easter Seal Society, Manchester, N.H.) describes him:

> At the beginning of each morning, the group is situated around a table as we begin the group language lesson. Tom [has] no idea of what is happening around [him]. Tom responds only when called upon and in most instances [only after I prompt with] two or three repetitions of the desired response.... Tom screens out everything, interacting only upon request and withdrawing back in his own world. [He] has an extremely short attention span and is able to answer 60% of the time correctly after being cued several times. Communication is extremely difficult. For example, when Tommy has reach-

ed his primary frustration level he purses his lips together and will pinch your arm. Peak frustration level involves crying and pinching, both of which subside almost as quickly as they came when interaction is halted.

His academic ability is beyond his apparent use for it: he is reported to flip quickly through the *TV Guide* and to have read and memorized all the TV specials and movies for the week. He also remembers details of car trips and map directions phenomenally well. His special interests are hand calculators and telephone books.

He was brought to the Logo Group with two other children from his class. My intention was to have the physical floor turtle ready, as its physical presence and real movement seemed more easily perceivable and less abstract than the screen drawings, but technical problems prevented its use. We had already set up some drawing programs to allow the children to make lines on the screen regardless of what keys they pressed on the teletypes. Tommy did not seem at all interested in the screen, but after pressing a few keys, seemingly at random, he began to type seriously. As he typed each letter, he would say the letter in a tense, strangely mechanically intoned voice.

METHUENMALL MACDONLADS BURGERKANG SEARS

He repeated the typing over and over, clearing the line if he made a typing mistake. He always repeated the same spelling errors. Although he never once pronounced any of the words he had typed, he continued to say every letter.

The computer crashed. I raced off to get it working again. When I returned, Tommy's teacher was trying to attract him back to the computer, but Tommy was heavily into a telephone book. "Ignoring" Tommy, I sat down at the computer and typed METHUENMALL. I read the word out loud and wondered audibly what word should follow it. Tommy left the telephone book open on the floor and sat on my lap, grabbed my hands, placed them on his stomach, and continued where I left off.

I began to recite the letters along with him. At first, I used my own voice, saying each letter with the slightly rising inflection that I normally use when listing things. My syllables were short, and each began louder than it ended. He continued his chant, each letter drawn out on one pitch, at one intensity, unchanged, and unchanging.

I decided to try the drone myself. When I copied his chant exactly, he reduced the tension in his voice. His syllables became shorter without being clipped, he dropped the intensity during the vowel, and allowed his pitch to drop, too. If I stopped speaking with him, he would go back to the mechanical drone. If I continued to spell with him, using my natural intonation while his voice was less tense, he would spell several letters in a clearly normal voice — one I had never before heard him use! He would return to the drone after a few letters, and, again, would stay droning if I persisted in using my normal voice or otherwise did not drone with him.

One time, during the spelling of BURGERKANG, he said the A with a very questioning voice. I said, "I?" and he cleared the line and typed the correct spelling. He got up, went over to the phone book, looked at it without touching it, returned to my lap and correctly spelled MCDON-ALDS. I might have guessed that the phone book had been open to that page all along!

Frequently, when he finished a word, he would flutter his hands in front of his eyes. He seemed pleased at these times. If I tried to copy that gesture he would grap my hands and place them on his stomach again. Much of the time, he rested his cheek against mine and occasionally, with apparent excitement, he took my hands and made them squeeze our two heads together gently.

Except for his clearing the screen (apparently to hide all of his past work and get rid of any mistakes he made), the computer was not much better for him than an electric typewriter.

Annette — A Frightened Girl

Annette is 14 years old. She is a pretty child with an engaging smile, bright eyes, and no visible handicap. She has severe language and moderate learning disabilities, including weaknesses in space perception, some apraxias, and astereognosis (poor tactile discrimination and/or recognition). She can match pictures of objects and reads at about a first-grade level, although with some marked syntactic weaknesses (as measured by arranging printed words into a sentence). Her speech is very limited, both in extent and clarity. I have not yet heard her say more than two words in a single utterance, but she enjoys signing and seems greatly to prefer it to speaking. Her record states that in a test situation that required her to respond verbally, she became frustrated and was twice near tears, but that in another testing situation when it was not necessary for her to talk, "she smiled a lot and really appeared to enjoy herself." She can add on her fingers and was learning the order of the alphabet the first time I met her. Although her diagnoses have included behavior disturbances and mental retardation secondary to brain damage, her language processing is so weak that it is difficult to be certain about the extent of her potential.

Annette goes slowly with everything. The most pressing problems, however, seem to be her disability with language and her low self-image as a learner, and we can deal directly with those problems. Using the computer, we can bypass the language problem by presenting the minimum language needed for the project desired. Although Annette can read, pictures or ideograms might be better than letters to minimize the threat that comes with anything academic.

Working with her was difficult, as she is very frightened by new things. She and I personally get along nicely, but she could not get near the computer without another girl, Linda, with her.

Linda acted as a kind of prosthesis for Annette, actually doing the typing while Annette gave the instructions. The roles they developed were especially intriguing, since Linda has a physical handicap but is far less academically retarded than Annette.

I attempted to continue working with Annette in this way, with her friend, but her teacher insisted she come alone to the next session (one must learn independence!). The consequence was that she would not try anything. Apparently she feared some kind of a test was involved. Just as Joey could interact with me only through the machine, Annette seemed able to interact with the machine only through a friend. Still, the interaction was real. She was designing the experiments and watching the results eagerly, two behaviors that are unusual for Annette and reveal aspects of her mind that are otherwise very much hidden.

Mental retardation is a term that refers, vaguely, to a low level of functioning. The notion that it is a unitary condition, "the cause" of the low level of functioning, is wrong, explains nothing, and impedes progress in the education of the mentally retarded. It would be delightful to discover that Annette's handicap is due to "nothing more than" the combination of severe language handicaps and associated severe emotional problems. From such a diagnosis, we could even entertain hopes of a "cure" — at the least, it would give us a better idea of how to treat her. Even if we cannot get a more detailed or accurate picture than that provided by the diagnosis of mental retardation, we need not be discouraged. Her problem, as opposed to our problem with her (and this really applies to every one of the children I have described, as well as to every child and adult I have not described), is having a rich, interesting, and estimable life, which must certainly be enhanced by seeing oneself as a communicator and an effector.

Although mental retardation is a much more common diagnosis than autism, I direct the rest of this chapter to a discussion of the more exotic handicap, partly because of my own greater personal contact with autistic children and partly because many of the issues of what to do with the cognitively handicapped child come into such sharp focus in the context of autism. Perhaps because the diagnosis of mental retardation is so much more common, our biases about it are too strong — we "understand it" too well. Our continuing tendency to regard autism as mysterious and exotic and to weave romances about the untapped mental powers and other psychic capabilities of the autistic child is, on balance, probably not very good for science. However, for the moment, it may actually free us to develop fruitful new insights about cognitive handicaps in general.

THE CHARACTERISTICS OF AUTISM

The performance of an autistic child is spotty. A simple act that he appears utterly incapable of performing is made all the more conspicuous by the graceful and routine performance of an almost identical task. A previously unknown and unrehearsed behavior will suddenly appear fully developed. An act that the child has clearly mastered will become impossible when some tiny and seemingly irrelevant detail of the environment is changed.

Although the handicaps of autism are not yet well understood, they are increasingly well identified and circumscribed. Wing (1972) has stated that

> [Autistic children have] a whole series of impairments of function and disturbances of behavior in addition to the social aloofness, obsessive desire for sameness, attachment to and skillful manipulation of objects and the muteness or non-communicative language which Kanner listed as the points of major importance. These additional problems included odd responses to sensory input (especially auditory and visual); preference for the use of touch, smell and movement to explore the environment; a tendency to use peripheral rather than central vision; severe limitation in comprehension of speech; abnormalities in spontaneous speech resembling those found in aphasia, in contrast to the marked ability to echo exactly other people's phrases; severe limitation in the comprehension and use of any non-vocal language such as gesture, mime, facial expression, the manual signs of the deaf, etc.; among those who could learn to read, an extraordinary discrepancy between good reading performance and very poor reading comprehension; marked inability to copy movements made by other people; problems in differentiating right-left, up-down, back-front; a tendency to abnormal stereotyped bodily movements; fascination with simple sensory stimuli, such as bright lights, spinning objects, mechanical sounds, tactile or even painful sensation, the last named sometimes leading to self injury; finally a remarkable ability to store memories of things exactly as they were first seen, heard or felt. (pp. 106–107)

It is important to try to distinguish, in this long list of the abnormalities of autistic children, between the problems that the autistic child has in dealing with his own life and the problems that we have in dealing with the autistic child.

Many of the handicaps listed by Wing seem of particular significance to the therapeutic application of a computer technology, as should be seen clearly when I describe a computer environment in detail for the autistic child (see Chapter 7). Three of these handicaps bear further discussion in order to dispel unhelpful, but popular, myths. The issues are: social aloofness; abnormalities of speech production, comprehension, and response to sound; and severe limitation in the comprehension and use of any non-vocal language. In addition there are two other issues: motivating the autistic child and considering the symptom as an adaptive effort.

Difficulties with Social Situations

The term *autism,* chosen by Kanner in 1943, expresses the importance he attached to the social aloofness of the children. Careful studies since about the mid-1960s make it difficult to accept autism as anything but a misunderstanding of these children. The observation that they are socially aloof is one of the best documented and most easily reproduced. The signs of this aloofness, their emotional unresponsiveness, lack of eye contact, and lack of response to the human voice, however, seem to be the results of handicaps in those modalities of dealing with their environment and are neither specific to their dealing with people nor indicative of a dislike for people.

Hermelin and O'Connor (1970) reported several studies dealing with the autistic child's response to people. The emotional unresponsiveness of autistic children is a conclusion based on their nonuse of expressive gestures, facial expression, and their apparent disregard of our use of them. A common example is the infant who does not reach out to be picked up in response to the adult's offer. Autistic children have difficulty copying or understanding any gestures (Hermelin and O'Connor, 1970) and that alone may explain their nonuse and unresponsiveness to gesture (DeMyer et al., 1972; DeMyer, 1976). In fact, Hermelin and O'Connor (1970) showed that autistic children were more aroused by and spent more time near people than various objects generally observed to be attractive to the children. The apparent avoidance of eye contact turned out to be a spurious result of shorter-than-normal gaze at anything. Hermelin and O'Connor concluded that, of the "two dimensions of social contact, physical distance and visual fixation...autistic children do not differ from normal and subnormal controls" (p. 118).

Difficulties with Verbal Language

In addition to his frequent unresponsiveness to sound, and his tendency not to discriminate speech sounds from other noises (Hermelin and O'Connor, 1970), the autistic child is noted to use an abnormal repertoire of nonverbal communicative sounds (Ricks and Wing, 1976) and to show an abnormal multiple response to sound (Condon, 1975). Hermelin and

O'Connor (1970) noted that the decoding and association abilities of autistic children were far more deficient via the oral/aural channel than via the visual/motor channel and that encoding processes (all output coding and not merely speech) were "grossly inadequate in all modalities tested" (p. 90). They found "severe impairment in the areas of grammatical and semantic aspects of language in autistic children, but normal responses to the phonological components" (p. 91). This is confirmed by their studies of nonverbal language and of social responsiveness. It is not that autistic children do not want to speak. It is that sounds do not have any meaning to them; sounds are just sounds.

Difficulties with Nonverbal Language

DeMyer et al. (1972) studied the ability of autistic children to imitate. One of their questions was motivated by the social aloofness issue: Is it that autistic children do not want to imitate people, or is it that they cannot? In their study, they observed autistic children in three different kinds of action situations, two requiring imitation:

Body Imitation (BI): "imitating examiner's body movement" (p. 269), such as touching one's nose or wiggling one's thumb.

Motor-Object Imitation (MOI): "imitating movements that examiner made with an object" (p. 269), such as kissing a doll or kicking a ball while seated.

Spontaneous Object Use (SOU): "giving the child an object and determining normatively his age level use of such object" (p. 269), such as zipping a zipper or putting pieces in a form board.

Autistic children were poorest in their body imitation and best in the spontaneous use of objects. DeMyer et al. (1972) have commented:

What makes imitation, especially BI [body imitation], so difficult to the [autistic] children? In order to imitate pure motor action, the imitator must remember a visual stimulus which leaves little or no trace on its environment, and then transfer the visual memory to the motor system. In contrast, in reproducing a MOI [motor object imitation] action, the imitator has some help in remembering such action because often some change has taken place that leaves an environmental trace. For example, if [the experimenter] covers a doll, the child has a model to copy in imitating [the experimenter]. (p. 280)

In the case of MOI, such as kissing a doll, that leave no model to be copied, the child has a concrete reference point (the doll) that does not leave his field of vision so that he can focus on this during the imitative act. In doing BI, the child has no such constant visual point of reference. Instead, he must focus directly on the movement itself which is a quickly disappearing change, remember it, and transfer the motion to his body part. To make this transfer,

he must not only possess a good visual memory but also have a clear idea that
his body is like the body of another.... (p. 281)

Spontaneous object use involved even less need for visual memory or
knowledge of body parts than MOI. For example, the forms of the Seguin
board and the matrix to which they are to be fitted remain in the visual field
of the child at all times. (p. 281)

When an infant or a child fails to remember the motor activities of his parents, or to relate such activities to his own body, then a smile, a wave of a
hand, or out-stretched arms would not attain cue value no matter how often
the mother's smile is paired with a positive reinforcer such as food or change
of diaper. In other words, the [autistic] infant or young child, unlike the normal or subnormal, could not utilize his parents' nonverbal communication
due to problems in remembering visual stimuli or transferring such stimuli to
his own motor system. (p. 283)

Although the autistic child's performance in all three kinds of imitation
was deficient, the retardation was relatively mild in the case of spontaneous object use, especially in comparison with body imitation. As difficult as it is for the child to learn on his own, it seems that it is even more
difficult for him to learn from others.

Can we set up a curriculum that is well suited to the child's "autistic"
way of learning? The computer provides such an opportunity and it is this
one feature — that the computer's use does not depend so much on imitation as on exploration — that seems to me to be the most likely explanation of the successes that I and others (Colby and Smith, 1971; Colby,
1973; Weir and Emanuel, 1976; Geoffrion and Bergeron, 1978) have felt.
This explanation is especially appealing in the light of the successful reports of two projects that in the implementation and use of the computer
are as vastly different from each other as are mine and that of Goodwin
and Goodwin (1969).

Can the Autistic Child Communicate at All?

Without verbal language and without nonverbal language, what else is
there? Can thinking go on? Yes, so the theory goes, as long as there is
some kind of internal symbolizing. But it is not yet very clear whether all
autistic children do symbolize internally. Ricks and Wing (1976) report
that the most severely retarded of autistic children "appear to have developed no concepts at all" (pp. 117-118). There are also some less impaired
children "who can, for example, match on size, colour or shape when
shown how by concrete demonstration, but who do not seem to have any
appreciation of even the simplest symbols in whatever sensory modality
they are presented" (p. 118). Ricks and Wing have concluded that

Abnormalities in the handling of symbols and in the development of language and other forms of communication are prominent features.... They may be the primary problems which explain all the other aspects of the syndrome, but, until more facts are available the question must remain open. (p. 134)

Wing (1976) has indicated one way of teaching an autistic child, which suggests to me a hopeful route for further research.

A very useful approach with autistic children is to teach the steps needed to accomplish practical skills by guiding the child's limbs through the necessary movements. An autistic child finds it difficult to watch other people perform and then translate the movements on to his own body; he cannot understand verbal instructions, but he can learn through feeling his own muscles move. (p. 201)

In addition to the kinesthetic communication, there is growing evidence that written communication, or other communication based on static visual symbols, may be helpful to the autistic child (Marshall and Hegrenes, 1972; Carrier, 1976; Wing, 1976). There is some encouragement that signed communication, taught through kinesthetic or other unorthodox approaches, may prove a usable system for autistic children (Miller and Miller, 1973).

Part of the problem, a part worthy of further research, is that the autistic child's lack of nonverbal as well as verbal language causes such a devastating intellectual as well as social isolation that one must expect a certain functional retardation to be secondary to that handicap. We know well the behavioral and emotional disturbances and mental retardation that can result in a deaf child whose deafness is not recognized early and who therefore lives for years in a world that he can neither fully understand nor talk back to. And the deaf child is missing only the verbal language information!

If the inability to form concepts or to use symbols is a primary handicap of the autistic child, the outlook is very poor. If the well-documented and numerous perceptual handicaps of the autistic child are there from birth, it may be that the observed conceptual handicaps are secondary to mental malnourishment. Intervention would then have to begin in infancy, much earlier than autism is now generally diagnosed.

Looking for the characteristics that might differentiate the autistic infant from others is a difficult task because determining the prevalence rate of autism (about 4 in 10,000) requires detailed massive screening, which is practical only where well baby visits are widespread and routine. What to look for presents another problem, but a discovery by Ricks and Wing (1976) suggests directions we might first explore.

English- and non-English-speaking mothers were asked to record vocalizations of their nonspeaking infants in four specific situations (Ricks and Wing, 1976). Four tapes, one of their infants, two of other English infants, and one of a non-English infant, were played for the English-speaking mothers. They were asked in each case to identify what situation evoked the baby's vocalizations, and they correctly did so for all four infants. They were also asked to identify the sounds of their own infant and of the non-English infant. This they could not do accurately.

The same technique was then applied using autistic children in place of the English infants and nonverbal Down's syndrome children in place of the non-English infants. Retarded children were used rather than normal children so they could be matched in age with the autistic children, autism not being generally diagnosed at an age when normal children are still totally nonspeaking.

The results were different. Mothers of autistic children could recognize their own child and the nonautistic child (whom they identified as normal!). Furthermore, each mother could "understand" the vocalizations of her own autistic child, meaning that each autistic child was consistent in the vocal expressions he used. They could not, however, understand the vocalizations of other autistic children, suggesting that the codes used by these children were highly idiosyncratic. All of the mothers understood the vocalizations of the "normal" (retarded) children.

Whether or not the autistic infant is already different in his vocalizations at an age when normal infants are still speaking their universal baby talk is not known. However, even if they are not, the transition age is probably earlier than autism is now generally recognized.

Sweet Motivation

Motivating the developmentally disabled child, especially the severely or multiply handicapped child, is often exceedingly difficult. It has been noted that deaf-blind children frequently remain unmotivated even by social or food rewards (Mira and Hoffman, 1974). Referring to the Mira and Hoffman study, Baker (1976) has stated

> Indeed, the most effective reinforcement proved to be allowing the child to engage in stereotyped behavior — the very interfering behavior which the teachers were seeking to eliminate.
> Similarly, the use of firm contingencies and punishment, difficult with any child, is often especially problematic for handicapped children's parents and teachers, who are apt to indulge these children in ways they would not treat a nonhandicapped child, with predictable consequences in unmanageable behavior. (p. 696)

A reinforcer that I have noted commonly in use is bits of chocolate or other candy, but Rimland (1972) reports research in the area of dietary effects on autistic symptoms and feels that there is evidence that sugar may exacerbate the autistic child's problems. While this research is, by Rimland's own admission, not yet conclusive, he argues that there can be little justification for feeding a child a suspected toxin just because the toxicity is as yet unproved. This conclusion, at best very weak from the standpoint of scientific research, takes on significance in the clinical domain. The relevance to the current writing is this: in the absence of activities that are intrinsically motivating to the autistic child, teachers and therapists have been forced to look for extrinsic motivational systems, including operant conditioning with candy rewards which may be toxic, and conditioning with aversive stimuli. Computers that seem to be intrinsically motivating to the autistic child, may provide a much-needed alternative.

AUTISTIC CHILDREN IN SCHOOL

Marshall and Hegrenes (1972) report work with an autistic child with no expressive verbal behavior.

> Initially Mark's behavior in the clinic was disruptive. It consisted of running around the room, lying on the floor, whining, hitting his head with his hands, attempting to leave the room, and kicking. In an attempt to gain stimulus control, the clinicians used a program of spatial organizers (various techniques to keep the child in a chair) and attending to the clinician. . . . A primary reinforcer (candy or ice cream) was used to establish sitting and attending behavior as well as eye contact. (p. 259)

In classes I have observed, a frequently used code word for reminding the child about eye contact was simply the command "Eyes!" This would often be followed by actually holding the child's head to establish eye contact. According to Marshall and Hegrenes (1972),

> Once these behaviors were established, imitative behaviors were introduced into the program. These included gross motor movements, oral posturing, and vocalization. Mark was not able to achieve criterion for vocalizations, and further attempts to elicit them resulted in disruptive behavior. (p. 259)

As well it ought to! In classes I studied, an autistic child would be shown a picture or object and the teacher or therapist would reward the child with a piece of candy if he says or repeats the name of the object.

If the observations are correct, that is, if autistic children tend to use peripheral vision more than foveal vision, if they are at their weakest in the oral/aural modality, and if their problems are exacerbated by sugar, then this procedure is no better than a cruel joke. We handicap the child's visual modality, force him to respond through an even weaker modality, and then, if he should happen to succeed anyway, we poison him. The little girl that Taylor (1976) describes as she recommends a more suitable practice sounds like she had previously been victim of the *Eyes!* command.

> It is often better for the teacher to sit to one side of the child. . . . Some children are disturbed by having an adult sitting facing them. They may glance at the teacher for cues instead of paying attention to the task. One little girl, instead of working, would stare at the teacher's face and say "Eyes, eyes." (p. 208)

THE SYMPTOM AS A HEALTHY, ADAPTIVE EFFORT

Educators of autistic children have often acted as if the only difference between an autistic child and a normal child is the autistic child's symptoms. Without regard to their usefulness for the child, many programs are designed to eliminate the symptoms as quickly and directly as possible. Prime targets of these behavior modification approaches are stereotypy, echolalia, and perseveration. Their indiscriminate extinction may have negative side effects.

Elkind (1967) has stated that

> One of the features of cognitive growth which Piaget and Montessori observed and to which both attached considerable importance, is the frequently repetitive character of behaviors associated with emerging mental abilities. Piaget and Montessori are almost unique in this regard since within both psychology and education repetitive behavior is often described pejoratively as "rote learning" or "perseveration." What both Piaget and Montessori have recognized, however, is the very great role which repetitive behavior plays in mental growth. (p. 541)

Elkind augments this observation with a study of his own that shows very neatly that "repetitive behavior . . . is frequently the outward manifestation of an emerging cognitive ability and the need to realize that ability through action" (p. 543).

Prizant (1978) argues that this "deviant" behavior frequently has an important function for the child and may, in fact, be an essential component in the child's language learning process. He suggests that "it may represent a child's attempt to maintain social interaction in the face of a severe communicative disorder" and that "indiscriminate extinction of all forms of immediate echolalia is ill-advised" (Prizant, 1978, pp. viii and x).

We may construe a repetitive behavior negatively as perseveration or "positively" as drill and practice; we may regard repetitive speech as echolalia or rehearsal. Labeling a behavior as pathological because it is different provides no new information about the behavior. Eliminating it rather than using it is wasteful.

As illustrations of how repetitive behavior may be interpreted as "intelligent," I offer two stories.

> Joshua was about 15 months old when he discovered how to turn the TV set on by pulling the knob. To give the set a vacation, his parents pulled the knob off the set and stuck it in the drawer of an end table. The drawer, although in Joshua's reach, was too difficult for him to open and he was forced to be creative about solving his problem. He recognized that the knob was an important part, so for some time he tried things like pulling other knobs off of the set and attempting to put them where the first knob had been. The dexterity and strength, not to mention knowhow, was beyond him and he consistently failed. Eventually Joshua succeeded in conquering the drawer in which the proper knob had been hidden. His father describes having watched in fascination as Joshua opened the drawer, removed the knob, carried it to the TV set, tried to make the knob stick in place, backed off, returned the knob to the drawer, closed the drawer and repeated the entire process over again five or six times. Each time, Joshua would put the knob back in the drawer, close the drawer and start all over again. It was as if Joshua were saying to himself, "Somewhere along the line, I am doing something wrong, but where?" As an elementary debugging technique Joshua tried repeating the same process in the hopes that whatever went wrong the first time would (magically?) go away. It is not a very sophisticated debugging technique, but then Joshua is just a beginner. This debugging technique is also part of our folk wisdom that never did develop the proverb "If at first you don't succeed, stop and figure out why." I might point out that schools which make a child repeat a grade that he has just failed and offer the same techniques the second year are not always showing much more sophistication than Joshua.

Joshua's perseveration was due to his dissatisfaction with the outcome of his previous trials.[11]

Gary, a deaf preschooler, demonstrates how perseveration can be the result of being satisfied with an outcome.

> In his first visit to the CARIS system, the computer was set to randomize the order of the elements in the noun and verb lists. During his first dozen trials Gary tried various nouns and verbs from different positions in the lists. He then settled into a seemingly perseverative pattern of always picking the first word on each list (Geoffrion, 1977).
>
> Is he perseverating or merely being economical? Since the order of the lists is randomly rearranged between each trial, there is no reason not to stick with the first item on the lists unless there is some particular picture he wanted to see more than another.
>
> Once Gary's pattern of always choosing the first word was noted, the computer program was modified to present the lists in fixed sequence. Gary's

---

[11]Marcus, personal communication, Artificial Intelligence Laboratory, M.I.T.

first choice, as might have been predicted, was again the first item on the list, but the second time the list appeared he shifted to a pattern that systematically explored all the nouns in the list. The fact that he recognized the repeated order immediately and also changed his behavior immediately suggests that his earlier behavior was not mindlessly repetitive. Both times he was doing all that was necessary to get an effect he liked — an interesting variety of pictures and animations.

Neither Joshua nor Gary is autistic, but our understanding of their perseverative behavior leads us to new interpretations of the behavior of Nancy, Joey, Kevin, and Thomas.

In his excellent study, Prizant (1978) found immediate echolalia to be serving social, facilitative, and communicative functions in many cases. Given what Piaget and others have discovered about the repetitive behavior of normal children, Prizant's findings indicate that through at least this modality, repetition, the autistic child has found a normal mode of communication.

The implications of this are clear. If, as we have seen, autistic children have little or no verbal or manual language, extinguishing their repetitive behaviors possibly destroys the only communicative ability that these children possess.

The computer's flexibility makes it a perfect extension for a child who is not flexible. We can give the child new opportunities for stimulation using whatever behaviors the child normally exhibits.

Part III
Special Technology

Chapter 6
Communicating with
the Computer

The computers I describe are capable of recognizing a fixed number of signals. We may assign these signals any particular meaning we like, e.g., letters, numbers, and punctuation, or whole commands. By teaching the computer to recognize and respond predictably to combinations of these symbols, we can increase its basic "vocabulary." For example, if the basic signals stand for letters, the computer can be taught to understand words, perhaps large numbers of them. We use this augmented vocabulary to build programs that further expand its abilities. Before I discuss how we may communicate letters, numbers, commands, or other information to the computer, it is helpful to see an example of this communication from the user's point of view.

DRAWING WITH THE TURTLE

Drawing is one of the computer-based activities most frequently used by the children discussed in this book. To understand better what the child actually does when drawing with the computer, let us follow the process of drawing a house. Figure 5 shows a TV-like display with a "scanning menu" at the left, a drawing screen on the right and an "echo area" at the bottom. The scanning menu is similar in operation to Susan's scanner (described in Chapter 3). Jane, for whom this scanner was designed, pressed a switch with her knee to indicate her choices to the computer as it offered them. (The drawings in this example were not made by Jane.) The wedge-shaped marker (cursor) in Figure 5 is pointing at FORWARD. Since the previous selection made by the child was the number 3, FORWARD 3 is echoed at the bottom of the display. The small triangle on the screen — we call it a "turtle" — follows instructions to create a drawing. The turtle indicates where one is drawing at any given time. It is currently facing up ("north") and would move in that direction if told to move FORWARD. It can also turn to the RIGHT or LEFT to face in another direction. The user must tell it how far to move FORWARD and how much to turn. Units were selected for convenience; FORWARD 1 moves the turtle about a centimeter, and RIGHT OR LEFT 1 turns the turtle 15°. When the screen is CLEARed, the turtle is set in the center facing "north". Figure 5 shows the turtle after it has gone FORWARD 3 and drawn a line to show its path.

The child next selects the number 8 (not shown) and waits for the cursor to reach the command LEFT. When that command is selected (Figure 6), LEFT 8 is echoed at the bottom of the screen and the turtle turns left 120°, that is 8 × 15. The turtle "remembers" the side and the angle separately so that one can conveniently draw without respecifying the dimen-

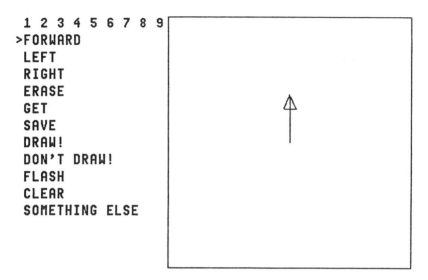

```
 1  2  3  4  5  6  7  8  9
>FORWARD
 LEFT
 RIGHT
 ERASE
 GET
 SAVE
 DRAW!
 DON'T DRAW!
 FLASH
 CLEAR
 SOMETHING ELSE
```

THE TURTLE'S PEN IS DOWN.

FORWARD 3

Figure 5.   The drawing screen and command scanner.

sions that remain the same. That is, if the child now commands the turtle to turn LEFT again without first selecting a new number, it will turn LEFT 8, as it did before. Similarly, FORWARD will continue to mean FORWARD 3 until another distance is indicated. Thus, after the original FORWARD 3 and LEFT 8, the sequence FORWARD, LEFT, FORWARD, LEFT now completes a triangle.

The child SAVEs the triangle as picture number 1 (Figure 7). In a similar manner, he draws and saves a picture of a square (Figures 8, 9, and 10). Note that when the angle was changed to a LEFT 6 (for the 90° angle), the new number had to be specified.

Figure 10 shows that the turtle ends up in the lower right hand corner of the square facing "east." This result was obtained by starting the drawing at the lower right, moving first toward the top and turning to the left at each corner. It would be more convenient if the turtle were to end at the top, since the next step is to get the triangle back and put it on the top to make a roof. In Figure 11, the child has CLEARed the screen and has rotated the turtle 90° to the left.

1 2 3 4 5 6 7 8 9
FORWARD
>LEFT
RIGHT
ERASE
GET
SAVE
DRAW!
DON'T DRAW!
FLASH
CLEAR
SOMETHING ELSE

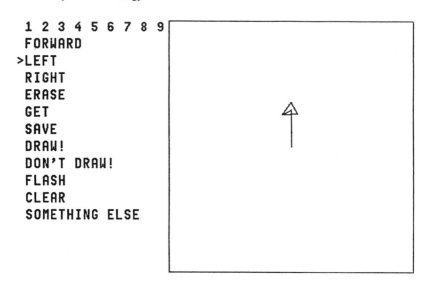

THE TURTLE'S PEN IS DOWN.

LEFT 8

Figure 6.   Turning the turtle left 120°.

1 2 3 4 5 6 7 8 9
FORWARD
LEFT
RIGHT
ERASE
GET
>SAVE
DRAW!
DON'T DRAW!
FLASH
CLEAR
SOMETHING ELSE

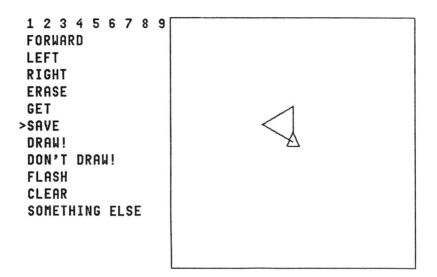

THE TURTLE'S PEN IS DOWN.

NUMBER 1

Figure 7.   Saving a drawing.

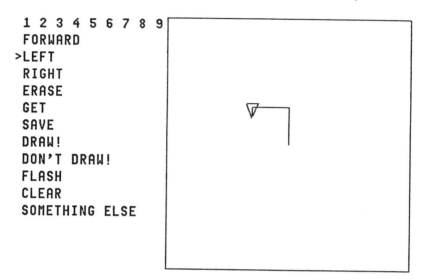

THE TURTLE'S PEN IS DOWN.

LEFT 6

Figure 8.   Two sides and two turns completed.

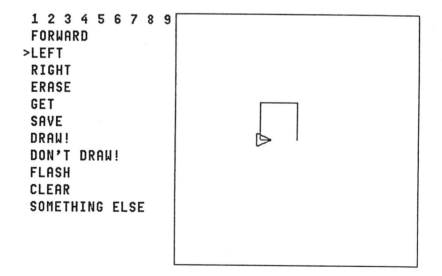

THE TURTLE'S PEN IS DOWN.

LEFT 6

Figure 9.   Three sides and three turns completed.

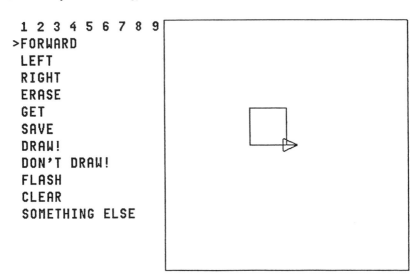

```
 1 2 3 4 5 6 7 8 9
>FORWARD
 LEFT
 RIGHT
 ERASE
 GET
 SAVE
 DRAW!
 DON'T DRAW!
 FLASH
 CLEAR
 SOMETHING ELSE
```

THE TURTLE'S PEN IS DOWN.

FORWARD 3

Figure 10.   The square.

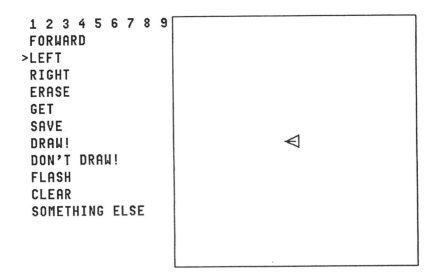

```
 1 2 3 4 5 6 7 8 9
 FORWARD
>LEFT
 RIGHT
 ERASE
 GET
 SAVE
 DRAW!
 DON'T DRAW!
 FLASH
 CLEAR
 SOMETHING ELSE
```

THE TURTLE'S PEN IS DOWN.

LEFT 6

Figure 11.   Starting the turtle facing "west".

Then when the child GETs picture number 2 (the square), it, too, is rotated 90° to the left and the turtle is now at the top (Figure 12). Simply GETting the triangle (Figure 13) has the wrong effect. The triangle is drawn exactly as it was when it was saved, so the house flips its lid. This problem is fixed by turning the turtle LEFT 2 (Figure 14) between GETting the square and GETting the triangle (Figure 15).

INPUT SCHEMES

For us to communicate with the computer, the basic signals it recognizes must be set out for us on some kind of menu. For the most part, choices are arranged in space and/or time. The scanning communicator is an example of arrangement in time.

Arrangements in Space

The choices are laid out in some convenient array with one switch per item and the user selects the items directly by activating the appropriate switch. A typewriter makes use of such an arrangement, where the information one can select includes numbers, letters, special symbols, spaces, etc.

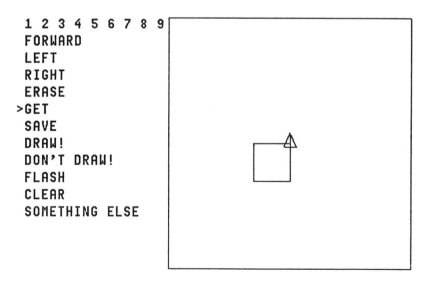

Figure 12.   Square with turtle at the top.

```
1 2 3 4 5 6 7 8 9
FORWARD
LEFT
RIGHT
ERASE
>GET
SAVE
DRAW!
DON'T DRAW!
FLASH
CLEAR
SOMETHING ELSE
```

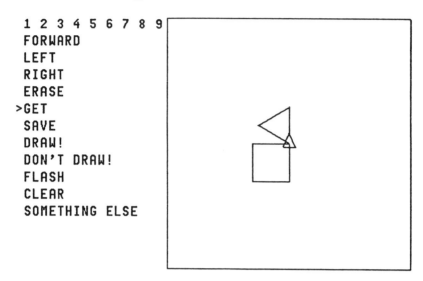

THE TURTLE'S PEN IS DOWN.

Figure 13.   House with a bug.

```
1 2 3 4 5 6 7 8 9
FORWARD
>LEFT
RIGHT
ERASE
GET
SAVE
DRAW!
DON'T DRAW!
FLASH
CLEAR
SOMETHING ELSE
```

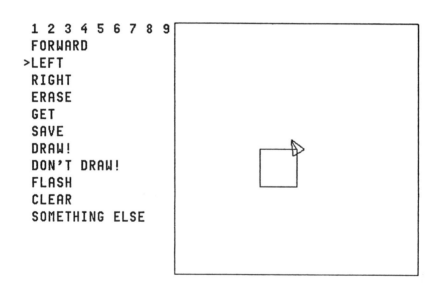

THE TURTLE'S PEN IS DOWN.

LEFT 2

Figure 14.   Square with turtle prepared to make a roof.

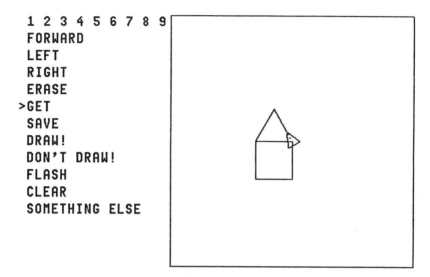

```
1 2 3 4 5 6 7 8 9
FORWARD
LEFT
RIGHT
ERASE
>GET
SAVE
DRAW!
DON'T DRAW!
FLASH
CLEAR
SOMETHING ELSE
```

THE TURTLE'S PEN IS DOWN.

NUMBER 1

Figure 15.   The house.

Each character has its own key. One aims and presses. (Automatic elevators also use this kind of input system.) The primary advantage of arrangements in space is that the user has random access to the choices. That is, he can get one choice as quickly and easily as another at any time. The requirements are that there be enough room for all of the options to be presented simultaneously and that the user have the ability to aim with adequate speed to make the selection practical.

Arrangements in Time

Arrangements in time have different advantages and drawbacks. Scanning systems do not require aim, as do arrangement-in-space schemes. Therefore, they are suitable for a person who lacks precise motor control. The principal disadvantage is that one does not have random access to the choices, but must wait for the desired choice to be presented.

Again, the choices are laid out in some convenient array, but this time there is only one switch controlling all of the choices. The switch is tailored to the needs of the user. The user may signal by bumping the switch with his hand or knee, or by blowing on it, or by making a vocal noise, or by flicking it with his tongue, or by letting a myoelectric sensor recognize the twitching of his eyebrow. Some kind of indicator (an arrow or a light) moves past each option and cycles back to the beginning when it has reached the end of the list. The user decides which option he wants and waits until the cursor indicates that particular option. The user then activates the switch, which selects that option and sends it to the computer.

Modifications of the basic idea can be made when needed. For example, we may wish to create a two-dimensional array of options and scan it by rows and columns to make the presentation of large numbers of choices fast enough to be practical.

Figure 16 illustrates one of the scanning systems used by the physically handicapped children in their work. The cursor cycles past the rows, allowing the user first to signal in which row the desired character is located. Then the cursor cycles within that row until the user sends another signal indicating the desired letter (Figure 17). In these illustrations, the order in which the letters were arranged was selected to minimize the waiting time for the letters used most frequently in drawing with LOGO. With all the letters and numbers available, the user has access to the entire LOGO language.

We generally did not present the full flexibility of the LOGO language on scanning communicators to children who were using the system for the first time. Instead, by presenting whole commands, we spared the child the tedium of laboriously spelling out each computer command.

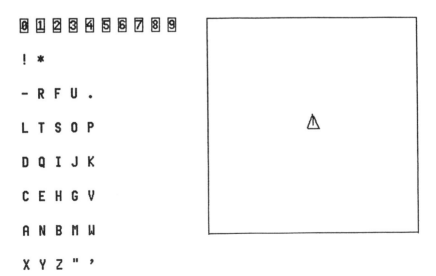

Figure 16.   Selecting the row of numbers.

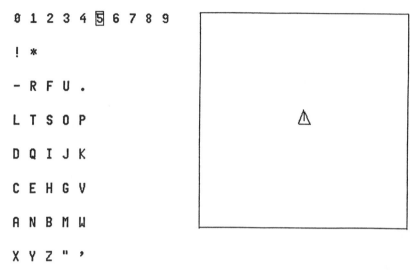

Figure 17.   Selecting the number 5.

This eventually would have been too restrictive, but it initially produced a very nice response-to-effort ratio. The communicator designed for Susan (see Figure 2, Chapter 3) used this principle.

TAILORING COMMUNICATION TO THE CHILD

In its simplest form, a scanning communicator uses only one input channel. However, there are ways to combine the advantages of both arrangements in space and arrangements in time.

If the child has more than one signal (e.g., a movement or sound) that he is capable of making, he can select from the computer's vocabulary using a code that represents each bit of information he wishes to communicate to the computer with some action or combination of actions. Thus with only 6 reliable signals, combinations of 2 of them uniquely identify 36 different items. As the number of his usable signals increases, the size of his vocabulary can be increased on the computer. This benefits the child in two ways. Easier access to more options is a benefit in itself. Furthermore, being able to make immediate functional use of a muscular act, which may not yet be adequate to serve the child in other ways, rewards that act itself by helping to practice and develop the skills that the child already has.

A physically handicapped child who, by reason of severe motor handicap alone, cannot speak, write, or type, might be provided with a communication board (McDonald and Schultz, 1973). Such an aid may offer the alphabet and, perhaps, some important phrases such as "I'm hungry," "I need to go to the bathroom," or "I love you." Alternatively, it might use photographs, line drawings, rebus representations, or special symbols systems, such as Blissymbols (Clark and Woodcock, 1976) or NonSLIP (Carrier, 1976), as a communicative code. If the child has any pointing ability with his hands, or if he can control his neck muscles well enough to point with a headstick or a tiny flashlight strapped to his head, he may communicate by pointing to the items on his board.

One limitation is immediately obvious. Mere pointing does not leave a trace, and thus the recipient of the communication must be standing nearby while the message is slowly composed.

There are still other problems. Although it is theoretically possible to compose any message on a board containing only letters and numbers, spelling is inherently slow and the use of a spelling board is really impractical for the child who, due to motoric impairment, cannot point quickly. A communicator requiring spelling is also of little help to the child for whom an orthographic representation of English is unfamiliar. The processes of acquiring spelling skills and producing text are slow and often frustrating. It is not an uncommon experience with the developmentally disabled child (as distinct from the child who has had expressive language and traumatically lost it) that he will make great initial progress working with a text-production device, then hit a low plateau and progress slowly or not at all thereafter. In the meantime, it becomes difficult to decide how much of the failure to progress is due to the child and how much is due to the method.

If the communication board presents only pictures or prepackaged phrases, its efficiency at delivering those messages is increased, but its flexibility is very low. Even combinations of the two approaches — menus containing useful phrases as well as the alphabet — do not fully solve these problems.

Some very clever improvements in the code by which the severely handicapped may communicate have been developed (e.g., Goodenough-Trepagnier's [1976b] PAR LE SI LA B) but the inherent physical slowness of the response forms generally chosen for current environmental control devices and communicators is a seriously limiting factor regardless of the code. The dimensions of this problem are sometimes startling. The ingenious way in which PAR LE SI LA B 'spells' French in whole syllables (rather than letters or phonemes) effectively reduces the physical effort required to spell a word by more than 60%. Still, at the estimated 1.5 pointings per word required by the PAR LE SI LA B system, a person who can point at the exceptionally fast rate of one syllable per second is only communicating at 40 words per minute, vastly slower than normal speech or even good typing. Scanning communicators are, of course, even slower.

The communication board is much better than nothing, but there is no comparison between any level of communication board competence and truly fluent sign language or speech. The computer provides a much more flexible aid to interpersonal communication, as it can change the menu of things to point at, allow the user to develop and store important abbreviations, and fill in structure words where the user has, for convenience, left them out. It can also be sensitive to a greater variety of impulses from the user, allowing him to select entries from the menu at a faster rate than if he had to point to each one separately. It enables the user to compose and edit a message without another person being present, and store the message until it is needed. Most important, the user can customize his computer-based communicator, as we tailor our language, to meet his needs. He need not be dependent upon another person to modify the board as some new event becomes significant in his life. The user's current menu can, and should, provide the necessary facilities to allow the user to change his own menu items, the scanning speed, and any other conventions he likes. With a computer that can be quickly and easily modified to the user's changing needs, the user, not the equipment, can decide what activities are most appropriate and appealing.

The importance of facile and unambiguous communication is well attested by normal experiences — our shyness at using a foreign language in which we do not feel fluent, our discomfort with stuttering, or our general agony with any form of severe speech impediment. If the computer takes an active role in the communication process, it may offer the needed facility and lack of ambiguity even to a beginning conversational partner.

Despite considerable support from the computer, conversation by text production may still be inappropriate for the beginner. A suitable code, such as an alphabet or syllabary, ultimately gives access to the entire range of sayable things, but to use it well, one must have something to say that is worth the effort. By contrast, we can offer a more limited menu, but one which can quickly be learned and used well for a computer-based activity such as drawing or music making. Becoming an expert, even in a miniature space, provides control and freedom rarely experienced by anyone, especially those identified as handicapped. The computer command menu does not provide a general social communication system, but does offer recreation, a source of independent activity. Providing a modality for communication does not guarantee its rich use, especially if someone has managed to do without it for a long time. The computer's independent generation of a concrete reason to communicate (e.g., to draw or play a game) may be the impetus needed for stimulating communicative efforts to take place at all. In view of this, I feel it is unfortunate that electronic aids to communication now depend so heavily on text production.

This observation strongly influenced the preliminary work out of which this book grew. I did not begin by trying to present full communication capabilities. Instead, we designed play opportunities that were academically and physically easy. Drawing on the video monitor and controlling the robot turtle were found to be particularly exciting to the children, perhaps precisely because they involve the control of movement. These activities require that the child learn a vocabulary of control commands, but the numbers, combinations, and meanings of these commands are more easily learnable in a short period of time than the numbers, combinations, and meanings of letters and words in free communication. Therefore, the effort that a child must invest before beginning to profit from his activity is reduced drastically.

The efforts are reduced, but the benefits are not small. Consider Susan's experience (see Chapter 3). In a short space of time, Susan learned to recognize a control vocabulary of nine printed words, learned their effects on the behavior of a robot "turtle," learned the behavioral effect of different numerical arguments to these commands, and for the first time in her life demonstrated that she was capable of planning and comprehending a complex sequence of instructions to bring about an intended result. These very same skills can be used, when Susan has the motivation, to expand her use of the computer in order to develop competence at even more complex tasks or social communication. In the meantime, play provides mental stimulation and begins to build a body of experience about which to communicate.

Jay and Jonny — Two Cerebral Palsied Adolescents

Jay is an 18-year-old spastic-athetoid quadriplegic with no use of his limbs and no useful speech. Setting up a system by which he could communicate with the computer was not straightforward. He was able to type with a headstick but made many typing errors during his first hour or so and it became clear that this was an inappropriate way for him to use the computer. Because he was capable of dealing with the full complexity of the LOGO language, we did not want to restrict his use of it with a command scanner. Yet a scanner seemed the obvious solution and so the one shown in Figures 16 and 17 was devised for him. He was apparently interested in trying it, but he preferred direct typing.

The greatest sources of his typing errors were in dragging the headstick over other keys after striking the correct key and in finding the delete key too inconveniently placed to make corrections easily. Not having a keyboard guard to protect him from the first kind of error, we decided to design a software keyboard guard. The drawing program he was using was modified so that each time he struck a key, the keyboard "went dead" for a second and therefore any keys he brushed by accident would be ignored. Furthermore, the program was instructed to interpret all the keys surrounding the delete key as if they, too, were delete keys, thus facilitating Jay's correction of his errors.

All this proved to be enormously helpful, but Jay surprised us the second time he visited the lab by typing with phenomenally greater accuracy and speed! Apparently, during the intervening week, he busied himself typing a lengthy letter to his parents describing the computer and had, in the process, taught himself some new control over his typing.

Facilitating communication with the computer was not the only problem we faced in teaching Jay LOGO. We were able to tell Jay whatever we wanted him to know, and whatever we might guess he wanted to know, but Jay had no effective means for communicating back to us. He had no way of asking us how to do a particular thing and rarely could we know what particular effect he was trying to achieve unless he was already far enough into a drawing for us to recognize it and anticipate the next move. Thus, we could not advise him in any useful way during his work. Furthermore, Jay had never received any formal instruction in geometry nor had he ever engaged in the knowledge-building experiences with dimension and angle that use of his arms or legs would have made possible. It thus seemed all the more critical that we missed his verbal feedback, since we could not tell, except for his experiments, what he did or did not understand. The crucial point is that his experiments were clear demonstrations of what was exploratory and what was planned and deliberated. He was able to demonstrate a high level of analytic and spatial ability, which was quite a contrast to the commonly held picture of him as being mentally retarded as well as physically handicapped.

During his first contact with the computer, Jay was taught the importance of the number 90 for right and left turns. He experimented with turns of other sizes as well, but used the 90° turns often enough to indicate he saw what was so special about them. He also played with different sizes of circles and different length lines, using both LC (a left-veering circle) and RC (a right-veering circle) to see the different effects. At one point he created a design that looked something like a butterfly whose wings consisted of randomly sized, nested circles. These experiments usually had lots of lines, turns, and circles in them, and were clearly exploratory.

After some initial experimentation with drawing on the TV screen, Jay taught the computer to repeat a procedure that he had invented. He cleared the screen, leaving the TV turtle facing straight up. He commanded it to go FORWARD 80, thus drawing a vertical line of length 80 (about 2 cm.). Jay then rotated the turtle 5° to the right with the command RIGHT 5. He looked at it for a long time, perhaps trying to see the nearly invisible effect of that turn. He then commanded it to rotate RIGHT 90°, thus facing it just 5° "south" of "east." He smiled. There are two commands that draw circles, one of which causes the turtle to veer to its left to draw the arc, and the other of which causes the turtle to veer to its right. Jay commanded the turtle to RC 90 (make a right-veering circle with a diameter of 90), but he did not like the result and so he erased it. He then gave the command LC 90 (left-circle) and named the procedure MOM (see Figure 18). The finished design looked like a lollipop — or to judge from its title, the head and body of a stick figure.

At the outset, this four-instruction procedure seems almost trivial, but there are several interesting observations that may be made about it.

Unlike his earlier drawings, this one was done with economy; that is, it was not a large conglomeration of effects, but a simple design done the simplest way. The changing of RC 90 to LC 90 indicated that he had a particular plan in mind and that he knew what kind of correction was necessary in order to achieve the plan.

The fact that he had that *particular* plan indicates even more. Had he made his RC 90 immediately after the line (FD 80) and without the intervening right turns, the circle would have been tangent to the line at its end, something like the letter "p" (Figure 19). If he then erased the RC and replaced it with an LC, his design would have looked like the design in Figure 20. But a lollipop's head and its stick are joined by a 90° angle (see

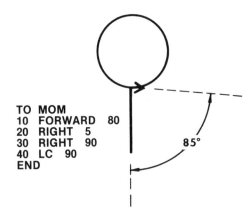

Figure 18.   TO MOM.

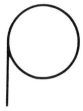

Figure 19.   FORWARD 80 RC 90.

Figure 20.   FORWARD 80 LC 90.

Figure 21). Jay introduced the angle without experimentation — he must have known in advance what was needed.

The angle Jay used was 95° and not 90°. The MOM procedure begins with the turtle facing "north" and ends with the turtle facing 5° "south" of "east." He typed MOM again while the first picture was still on the screen. This time the turtle began facing 5° "south" of "east" and ended 10° "west" of "south." Two more MOMs completed a new procedure that he named GOING (Figure 22).

Could he have known that if MOM's lollipop angle were exactly 90°, GOING would have closed to make a square with circles at its corners? The fact that it did not make a closed figure made it useful for creating an even more elaborate design. He compounded eight GOING's into a procedure and named it DADS (Figure 23) and combined three DADSs to make a procedure that he named JAY (Figure 24).

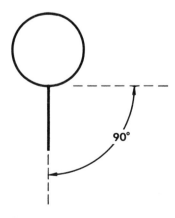

Figure 21.   FORWARD 80 RIGHT 90 LC 90.

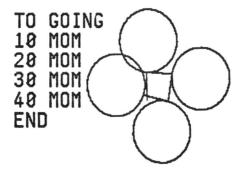

```
TO GOING
10 MOM
20 MOM
30 MOM
40 MOM
END
```

Figure 22.   TO GOING.

It is difficult to know what personal meanings there were in his choice of designs or the names he chose to give them, because Jay could, at best, *show* us what was going on in his mind; he could not tell us what we were not smart enough to ask in yes/no form.

Other children were also able to make it clear that the projects that they were engaged in were personally meaningful to them. For example, Laurie, a 12-year-old girl who loved design and symmetry and who had never drawn before, produced the design in Figure 25.

Jonny is a bright, friendly 14-year-old with athetoid cerebral palsy. His speech is labored but usually understandable. His arm and hand control are insufficient for all but the most gross movements. He expresses his frustration at not being able to draw. He talks comfortably of his abilities and disabilities, and is just as sensitive to those of his schoolmates. ("Do you know Jay? He's even more spastic than I am!") Often as we worked together, he would make a suggestion about how to build or ar-

```
TO DADS
1 GOING
2 GOING
3 GOING
4 GOING
5 GOING
6 GOING
7 GOING
8 GOING
END
```

Figure 23.   TO DADS.

```
TO JAY
1 DADS
2 DADS
3 DADS
END
```
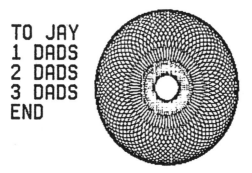

Figure 24.   TO JAY.

range a device for another child, and he is particularly interested in designing aids for cerebral palsied persons. He controls his own electric wheelchair, but he would prefer a non-electric one ("I don't get enough exercise with an electric wheelchair"). Standard hand-powered wheelchair designs have proved impractical for him, but he has invented one that he feels would be quite suitable. Although he can imagine the design of the chair, he cannot draw it. "Just give me a week with someone who will draw for me and I will tell him exactly what to draw." Jonny's first attempt at drawing on the computer did not show the technical details he could describe, but it showed *him* that drawing such details was not impossible (see Figure 26).

Cheryl — "It talks to me"

Not all children want to draw pictures. Some, and not necessarily the ones that we would predict, enjoy the verbal communication possibilities of the

Figure 25.   Laurie's design.

Figure 26.   Jonny's first drawing of a wheelchair.

computer. Cheryl was a normal sixth-grader from a local public school. She was a poor reader, had repeated a grade, and was, in general, on the bottom of the academic heap. I assumed, because of this, that she would most like the physical turtle, the least school-like thing we had. She did enjoy typing instructions to it and having it obey her, but she became much more interested when it "talked back" to her. Once she typed 100 without having indicated whether the turtle was supposed to go forward 100 or turn 100°. The computer replied

YOU DIDN'T SAY WHAT TO DO WITH 100.

Cheryl labored to read the message and turned to me and said, "How can it do that? That turtle is more like a friend that a machine. It talks to me!" When offered the prospect of teaching it to say more things, Cheryl's excitement grew.

During our next session I showed Cheryl how she could teach the computer to compose sentences from words of her own choosing. She decided to make a gossip column. She began by creating a list of all the names of the children in her class and a list of suitable actions (e.g., kisses, sits on, hates, makes out with, bites, loves, hits). She instructed the computer to select items at random from these lists and then to combine them as subject, verb, and object of a sentence. After printing the sentence, the computer was to repeat the whole cycle. When she finally got her program working, she generated enough gossip to paper her walls! Interestingly, she and Frank, a friend with even more severe reading difficulties than she, both spread out on the floor and read through the column, line by line, putting stars next to the sentences they liked. Cheryl was particularly delighted when the machine typed MARC LOVES CHERYL. She told me quietly, but only after the machine had already spilled the beans, that Marc was her boyfriend.

Aside from the pleasure that Jay, Laurie, Jonny, and Cheryl derived from doing their projects and the obvious pride they felt when their procedures worked, one aspect of these four examples that ties them together is the highly communicative and personal nature of the projects. Jay's drawings were his communication link with us. That he made the drawings for the purpose of communicating is highly unlikely, but he could tell that we recognized the planning that went into his work, and he appeared pleased with our discovery. This is the first step in setting up an effective communication channel. Laurie, who loved symmetry, showed us an example of her mental designs. Jonny, of course, had told us how much he wanted to draw a picture of a wheelchair, but the communication did not feel complete to him until he could also show us his ideas. For Cheryl, the computer was a mouthpiece that could say things she did not want to have to take full responsibility for. A sensitive observer may find unintended communications in almost any action, but the computer is the information-handling system par excellence. Its every action is a reflection of its user's wishes. It provides the power and stimulation to engage in a wide variety of activities. It allows choice to explore geometric design or social fantasy. Cheryl's procedure created a lot of reading for her, an activity that is associated with her long history of academic failure, yet she had controlled the vocabulary of her reading, and guaranteed that the content would be interesting. The fact that she so totally externalized her fantasies to the machine became evident as she starred the sentences that said what she meant — sentences she was reluctant to say alone. The fact that she wanted them communicated was clear when she hauled me over to look at the sentences she had starred.

Observing the child as a computer programmer allows us to see aspects of the child's mind that are otherwise generally invisible. We see not merely the child's ability to read, but his ability to come up with an idea and generate a plan for realizing it. We see the child at play.

Chapter 7
Novel Sources of Control,
Activity, and Meaning

With the number of severely handicapped children and youth estimated to be in the millions and the urgency of providing an "appropriate free public education" (not to mention other life opportunities) ever more apparent, it becomes essential that we investigate not only innovative techniques that facilitate or accelerate the attainment of goals we now see as possible but also those techniques that promise to open up vast new possibilities. Microprocessor technology offers educators, habilitation personnel and human factors engineers a fertile ground for designing prosthetic and educational devices with a range and power previously unknown. The limited adaptability of pre-microprocessor technology not only restricted what we could build, but constrained our imaginations as well.

The computer's potential value varies with the child for whom it is intended. For the physically handicapped child, the computer can be a genuine prosthetic device, providing the child with control where he had none before.

The deaf child's needs are different. Assuming a healthy social situation that includes peers and adults with whom the child can comfortably interact, the deaf child lives a very normal life, except where difficulties with English have restricted the information that the child has or can get. I do not see a computer making up for the unhealthy social situations that deaf children frequently find themselves in, nor do I see it as a substitute teacher of English. However, the computer makes a contribution by providing activities that motivate genuine use of English, fostering its development, and that supplement other interpersonal experiences with the language. Beyond that, the computer should provide intellectual challenge independent of English competence for the usual purpose that intellectual challenge serves — to help keep these children's healthy minds from becoming flabby. Fantasy games (such as the one described later) and computer programming, itself, are among the richly engaging sources of mental stimulation that computers can help provide for a deaf child as a supplement to very human interactions.

For the autistic child, also, physical control is not the issue, nor is his problem with English, per se. Rather, the issue is that all conventional communication is disrupted for the child. For the physically handicapped child, the computer is potentially a lifelong prosthesis. For the deaf child, the computer may be more a temporary educational aid, although some lifelong applications are described in the text. For the autistic child, it is not yet clear which of these two functions is most appropriate for the computer to serve. At a minimum, the computer may simply be the nervous system of a sensitively responsive recreational device that is physically engineered to be indestructible and is tucked in the back wards of institutions to relieve the boredom of the residents. That, to me, seems both an underuse of our imaginations in designing human living conditions and an underuse of the potential power of computers. With thoughtful design, the computer may be able to bridge the communication gap for the autistic child by adapting to the child's communicative abilities rather than requiring the child to adapt to ours.

The purpose of this chapter is to outline some very specific ways in which computers may be adapted for each of these groups of people.

NOVEL SOURCES OF CONTROL
FOR THE PHYSICALLY HANDICAPPED CHILD

The basic concept of biofeedback — providing feedback that is normally unavailable — is a highly productive one. The profound limitations in activity and social communication that result from expressive problems are obvious, but as I have stressed before, one of the most serious consequences of motoric disability is the loss of feedback, a loss that may retard social, cognitive, and even perceptual-motor development, further compounding the handicap. Techniques originally developed for biofeedback offer great promise as a way to communicate with a computer.

Previous Conceptions of Feedback

In the past, biofeedback has been used to:

Train or retrain muscles to perform a complete and functional coordinated act. For example, Nickerson et al. (1976) provided visual feedback to deaf students in order to aid the development of voice control for speech. Brudny et al. (1974) used EMG feedback to help patients develop functional use of their limbs. Harris, Spelman, and Hymer (1972, 1974) have used simple feedback devices to help athetoid patients remember to control various aspects of their posture, e.g., head position. In each of these situations, the goal of the feedback is to train the person to perform a complete act that is later to be used in the absence of the feedback device.

Develop control over bodily systems not normally considered to be under conscious control. For example, biofeedback has been used to help patients eliminate bruxism, control hypertension, and prevent or relieve tension headaches.

Provide a control modality for certain severely physically handicapped individuals who have insufficient limb control to command control devices conveniently in other ways. In these cases, the patient is learning to control a muscle that is perhaps never normally used for communication or activity and that, in some cases, may not already be under conscious control (similar to the application immediately above). Generally, myoelectric signals are used in some fashion (most often, they simply trigger a switch) to control a device that then serves as an aid or environmental controller. Unlike the two previously mentioned applications, control over the selected muscle is of no value unless the equipment is attached. Like the first application (but unlike the second), the purpose of the learning is to affect something external to the individual himself.

A distinctly different application for enhanced feedback involves providing a genuinely creative use for a modality that a child already can control but cannot control well enough for normal use.

Three modalities that appear to be very promising as high-bandwidth channels for communication (via direct or coded selection) use vocal, myoelectric, or limb movement signals. The techniques I describe endeavor to be the synthesis of the exercise and substitution models of therapy I discussed in Chapter 2. The techniques seem likely to improve these modalities with use and to develop functional value to the handicapped person in ways far removed from the communication device to which they were first applied.

Two modalities that I chose not to describe in depth — eye control and head/neck control — do deserve brief mention. Eye tracking is, in some ways, a natural initial choice for communication devices. It is often the case that a severely involved cerebral palsied person will maintain gaze control even when nearly all other voluntary muscle control is lacking. Successful use of line-of-sight communicators has been made and electronic eye-tracking devices are reliable sources of control. Eyes, however, have been optimized as input devices, not output devices. Restricting where a person may look while communicating, or worse yet, forcing a constant shifting of gaze in connection with the spelling rather than the dynamics of the conversation, has serious shortcomings. While research in the use of eye-tracking and line-of-sight devices should certainly continue, other channels that yield the same capacity without the undesirable side effects of tying up the input channels and restricting eye contact must also be vigorously pursued.

It goes almost without saying that the headstick is a less that optimal technology for controlling a computer. Aside from tying up the eyes again, this time by forcing head movement and eye compensation, there is some discomfort, not to mention a cosmetic problem, in wearing a headstick all the time. Some people find it impossible to use a headstick at all.

The Vocal Channel

Inexpensive devices that are capable of learning to recognize the user's vocal productions now exist. They can serve as input to a computer that can then respond in a unique way to each distinct vocalization. With such a system, even a nonvocal individual can have direct control over a computer, provided he or she can reliably reproduce at least a few vocal noises.

Jane is one such person. Except for the few hours per week that she might exercise her six to eight sounds for the speech therapist, there is little use she can make of her vocal ability. Because nothing important to her ever depends on her carefully differentiating these sounds, even her periodic vocalization does not serve to exercise or develop that ability. However, if her "speech" could be made to serve a useful function, and if every time she became capable of making a new sound, that sound could immediately be put to work, then she would have a powerful incentive to practice the distinctions that she is already capable of making and she would have a motivation to develop new skills. The practice itself might foster the development of the new skills.

With a vocal input device installed in her wheelchair, Jane can begin to use her vocal capabilities for communication or control purposes, e.g., to drive her wheelchair, to play a game, or to cause a voice-producing device to say the words she had wanted to say with her own mouth. A very small repertoire of sounds can be used in coded selection of a considerably larger number of choices. For Jane and many others, producing these vocal acts, despite their insufficiency for speech, can be much easier than limb or head/neck control and perhaps less problematic than using eye control.

The immediate benefit is the new channel for control this may provide Jane. A secondary benefit comes from the feeling that her voice was adequate to the task.

There are still other potential benefits that need to be researched. I hypothesize that consistent use of a vocal control system would lead to better vocal control seen specifically in:

An increase in the number of distinguishably different vocal sounds
An increase in the reliability of the child's attainment of the desired machine response[12] (improvement on the hit-to-miss ratio)
A decrease in the latency period between vocalizations, reflected both in a decrease in time before the child is capable of producing a new vocal-

---

[12]Disarthric speech tends to be consistent. Some improvements in reliability (as distinct from the number of sounds) would be a function of a combined effort of child and teacher to tune the system to the child's characteristic volume and the ambient noise. Still, the child's part in this process is significant. Volume, speech rate, and intent influence the "hit-rate." The most fundamental task facing some children will be that of assigning meaning to a physical act (in this case speech) which is the first step toward acquiring expressive language. This may well not be a trivial task for many children for whom conventional expressive ability has been lacking.

ization and in an increase in the child's use of the vocal channel for control

Thus, use of vocal sound recognition as a channel for environmental control and communication promises to be a valuable adjunct to conventional speech therapy. An exciting, if optimistic, possibility is that of developing vocal control sufficient to permit a computer mapping from the individual's vocalizations to standard English speech. Unlike the orthographic representation of English, text production, this kind of feedback would use an aural phonetic representation of English, computer generated speech — a communication medium with which the hearing child is already familiar.

Tracking Limb Movement

Susan, like many other athetoids, is capable of directing her hand to a particular point, but she does not have the motor control to make that movement smoothly, directly, or precisely. She is also not always able to come to true rest at that point. As a result, even though she can exercise arm control, there are few activities that she is capable of doing that make use of that control. An important point to remember, however, is that her limited successes are signs that she is sending correct signals. Her problem is that she is unable to prevent noise from accompanying them.

It is possible to enhance the feedback that a person such as Susan can gain from her arm movements by employing the path as well as the terminal point of her arm motions. Using an electronic data tablet that senses the position of a stylus on its surface, we can represent the position of Susan's hand as it moves over the tablet by tracking its movements with a cursor on a video monitor (see Figure 27). Instead of tracking her hand movements exactly, that light point may anticipate her hand in movement, providing predictively speeded feedback, or it may follow a path representing a first-order integration of her hand's trace on the tablet. In these latter cases, Susan's control over the cursor increases. Sophisticated ways of filtering noise out of the signal may be chosen to increase Susan's control over the cursor even more. Although typing to the turtle already provides Susan with access to drawing, the tablet interface is psychologically more direct. Furthermore, it furnishes filtered, enhanced feedback that should allow Susan to further develop the physical control that she already has.

Susan experiences garbled proprioceptive feedback — inapproprioception (Harris, 1971). Because perceptual-motor systems are constrained to keep themselves in tune through consistent and active feedback (reaf-

Figure 27.   Electronic data tablet.

ference) and because only some of Susan's movements are consciously willed, she may be getting such inadequate feedback that, were her athetosis miraculously to disappear, she would still have to learn perceptual-motor integration. Techniques like those mentioned above can enhance the signal and filter out the noise in Susan's attempts at a straight line, and thus can be used to provide feedback. This feedback may allow her to develop her perceptual-motor integration and thereby help her perform limb movements more accurately, despite the continued interference of the basic defect that causes the constant and regular writhing of her muscles. There is evidence that enhanced feedback can greatly improve the physical skills of the athetoid person. Speech skills, despite their enormous complexity, have been shown to respond to feedback enhancements. Berko (1975) has reported

> Outstandingly remarkable speech improvement...with about 60% of 200 children thus far tested. The noted improvements include improved specific articulation, better general intelligibility, and, in some cases, the tendency to use speech more freely when using the EAF [enhanced auditory feedback] device than when speaking without it. Some youngsters who normally rarely speak at all, make frequent speech attempts when using EAF. It would seem that the psychological effect of having a successful speech experience encourages further speech attempts. (p. 25)

Current EAF devices are no larger than a pocket calculator. Not only are speech improvements noted during EAF use, but they carry over for a period of time when no apparatus is used. Research is being continued by Lencione at UCLA (Berko, personal communication). Again, functional habilitation is a byproduct of functional use.

Basic and clinical research opportunities abound. Computer enhancement of pointing resolution may allow the development of better direct-selection communicators (arrangements in space). One might also use the tablet to study the development of certain physical skills such as the ability to track a slowly moving target.

With use of the tablet, I would expect the accuracy (resolution) of pointing to increase, the skill at producing a desired computer-enhanced line to increase, and tracking ability (i.e., feedback-mediated movement rather than ballistic movement) to improve.

The Myoelectric Channel

Myoelectric signals may ultimately offer the best source of control for some individuals, spastic individuals in particular. At first thought this may seem implausible, since the neuromuscularly impaired person's handicap should interfere as much with the signals read off contracting muscles as with the muscles' behaviors themselves, but there are some circumstances in which this is not the case.

The difficulties that a spastic person like Jane has in moving her arms are primarily due to the interference of unwanted reflexes. To the extent that she is able to make any progress at all in the right direction, she is sending some of the correct signals to the agonist muscles. The interfering reflex is evoked by stretching the antagonist muscles. When she is relaxed and does not move her arm, she does not excite the reflex responses. If a weak enough neural signal is then sent, so weak that her arm remains motionless, that signal will not evoke reflex reactions. We should then be able to recognize her signal with a myoelectric sensing device. Under these circumstances, there is no obvious difference between the spastic and the normal individual.

Most intriguing is the possibility that a spastic person can learn an efficient multi-muscle task equivalent in bandwidth to high-speed typing. Every reported successful clinical application of EMG feedback has been predicated on the notion that the patient can develop control over a specified muscle within a reasonable, usually short, period of time. That such control can be exercised even over pathological neural processes may be seen in Harris et al. (1972, 1974); Amato, Hermsmayer, and Kleinman (1973); Kleinman et al. (1975); Brudny et al. (1976); and Finley et al. (1976).

After integrating the raw signal from a single muscle, the myoelectric variables available are the amplitude and duration of pulses and the interval between them. Different combinations of these can encode a fairly rich set of commands that can in principle be executed by a single muscle. Preliminary experiments with myoelectric control of drawing were done with two normal 8-year-olds in the Logo laboratory. The greatest difficulty we had in teaching them to draw while motionless was in getting them to sit still! They needed to practice about 15 minutes before they could reliably control the turtle. It remains to be seen how much resolution in control is possible for the spastic individual and what kinds of multi-muscle combinations are usable. The possibilities for the spastic person to make use of this modality for control appear just as good as for the normal person.

Summary

The greatest benefits of the computer for the severely physically handicapped child are in the area of control. Social communication is only one aspect of this. With the flexibility and affordability of off-the-shelf microprocessors, we for the first time have the chance to open up a world of much more normal experiencing to the severely physically handicapped child, thereby removing many of the handicaps now associated with physical disabilities.

Research grounded in the belief that physical and mental skills are highly similar has produced some observations that lead to a new understanding of the development and facilitation of physical skills. For instance, people at the Logo Group (Austin, 1974) have taught others to juggle without either touching them or demonstrating the skill. The notion that a complex physical procedure such as juggling can be decomposed into smaller easy-to-learn subprocedures and can be communicated verbally has a message for the habilitation of Jane and children like her. Locating an object in space and grasping it is a complex procedure. We can see babies practicing the "primitives" and subprocedures which, combined properly, will lead to reaching and grasping.

What about a child like Jane? Such a child gets inadequate feedback either because she cannot make enough of a movement to get clear visual and proprioceptive information back or because extraneous movement is occurring that makes it difficult for her to determine what part of the feedback is signal and what part noise. Teachers and therapists who have a clear understanding of how physical skills are built and who can provide accurate sensitive feedback may be able to help Jane learn to reach and grasp much the way I could learn to juggle. The fact that reaching and grasping are not "natural" to her may be no more of a hindrance than the fact that juggling is not natural to me.

Although this is an application of the hospital model, both the immediate and the far-reaching goals are of great value to children such as Jane and Susan. Unfortunately, some of the risks of the hospital model still apply and it is worth trying to avoid those risks. As liberating an experience as it is to gain new control of oneself, it must have even greater significance to see that one can immediately use this self-control to have predictable and desired effects on one's environment. Severely physically handicapped persons are prevented not only from writing and feeding themselves, but also from playing, which for normal children is an enormous source of informal learning and one that should be stressed in the design of activities. In order for these children to communicate with the computer, they must perform some voluntary act. By choosing sensitively among the acts that these children perform, we can find acts that allow them the optimal access to the computer and communication, and that help them practice muscular acts that can be the subprocedures that the child may one day be able to combine into a complex physical act. We are not sugarcoating an exercise to make it fun, but are taking an enjoyable and beneficial activity and adding another free benefit to it. The philosophical distinction, I believe, is important.

NOVEL SOURCES OF ACTIVITY FOR THE DEAF CHILD

Of the values of the computer that are specific to the deaf child, probably the greatest is its potential to be a flexible and growing source of intellectual stimulation that encourages, but does not depend on, social communication. Once the child understands the elements of the simple computer language, it is possible for him to create and carry out a project that is more complex than he could easily communicate to another person. For both deaf and hearing children, this creates a situation of peak motivation because the project is their own special invention. Activities that involve drawing and movements in space are ones at which the deaf child has no handicap at all. The signing deaf child, in fact, is very much at home in a visual world, and has become quite accustomed to assigning names to particular places, and places to particular names. Even the gossip column project that Cheryl tried might be as interesting to a deaf child as it was to Cheryl, and the motivation to be in control of language rather than controlled by it might even be higher.

As the computer is a context for activities that engage the child's intellect and stimulate his sense of fun, it can offer intellectual activities worth talking about without requiring that the child work through his weakest link, his deficient English. The particular limited language of the computer is no more new to the deaf child than it is to the hearing child, and our initial experiences with deaf children have closely paralleled the experiences that have been reported with hearing children (e.g., Papert, 1971a, b, 1973).

Although there are other routes that we have used, the principal mode for the deaf child's communication with the computer is through typing. Aside from gaining a presumably pleasant experience with composing letters into words, the child is producing names to refer to events he has caused (programs he has written), ascribing meaning to these names, and developing the machine's vocabulary. These are important as both mathematical and linguistic experiences. Although he is not constrained to spell his new words "correctly," he must spell them consistently. Experience has shown that this does not reinforce wrong spellings, but instead tends to raise the consciousness that words have spellings and encourages the children to ask about and use conventional spellings.

Perhaps the most important educational interventions for the deaf child are the things that help to develop his weak English. Recalling Brennan's (1975) caveat against a "a purely imitative model of language acquisition" and her warning against "denying the child the opportunity to construct his own language," we must be wary of creating computer-aided instruction (CAI) that, like the typical schooling of deaf children, seriously compounds their problem of learning English by perpetuating the abnormality of their experience with written English.

Wilbur (1977) has clearly stated the warning that

> The study of language within a pragmatic framework includes contextual environments larger than the sentence, such as the paragraph or conversation. . . . The problem [of deaf English] most likely arises from the heavy em-

phasis that is placed on the proper structure of the *single sentence* in language training programs for the deaf. . . . As long as the modifications in syntax that arise from pragmatic context are ignored in language programs, deaf student's facility with English will continue to be stilted and stereotyped. (p. 86, italics mine)

Conventional conceptions of CAI language systems for deaf students have concentrated almost exclusively on intra-sentential constructions (e.g., Galbraith, 1978).

The message of these two scientists, Brennan and Wilbur, is especially important to educators of the deaf concerned with the development of computer-based instructional systems. We must de-emphasize right-wrong, S-R, multiple-guess lessons and instead emphasize the communication component of writing. We must deal with units larger than phrases. We must take advantage of the natural tendency for people to play with their own language.

A final point should be made about the deaf child's acquisition of English. Although the hearing child has only an ephemeral (spoken or signed) representation of his language for several years, he has had lots of language play opportunities which the deaf child has lacked in English. With the importance of language play in the acquisition process (cf. Athey, in press), we should aim computer activities for the deaf child specifically toward play.

There are more opportunities for language play when one has lasting (written or taped) expressions to use as well as ephemeral ones. Writing affords the means to compose and revise thoughts. It is a medium for exploring relationships and alternate means of expression.

For the deaf person, written English has additional significance. Writing allows self expression in English without time pressure, a relief to any nonnative language user. Writing facilitates communications with the hearing population for social, educational, and business purposes. It is a primary source of current information for a person who cannot use the radio or telephone.

The Computer as Animated Scratchpad

Before considering needs that are specific to the deaf student, we should understand how a computer editor influences anyone's production of a text.

With conventional writing technologies (that is, with pen, eraser, and typewriter) a great deal of time and energy is spent on the physical activities involved in text production. In schools, this means that we judge the quality of a student's writing on the basis of what he is capable of producing after two, or at most three, drafts. The teacher cannot realistically demand successive corrections of the same document because of the time involved. With the computer, it would be possible for a student to update a draft a few dozen times with the same expenditure of effort that previously had been required for two drafts alone.

Without the computer's ability to store and edit text, each change to a written or typed composition defaces it and requires that it be rewritten or retyped before handing it in. This puts a premium on catching all errors early and not making many changes after the first draft's corrections have been neatly typed into a second, generally final, draft. Complex changes made in editing a draft are likely to introduce new problems as the old ones are eliminated. Some people can do much of this work in their heads just as some people can picture a room with the furniture rearranged; others cannot. They need the feedback from seeing intermediate stages before they can evaluate and continue the progress they have made. Practical constraints limit the time and effort one can expend on trial arrangements, whether of furniture or text. With the computer, each correction requires only the typing of the correction itself. This ease in correcting a document makes it highly worthwhile to search for further improvements and provides the time within which to make those corrections.

A computer text editor is not an active agent. It is an electronic scratchpad and makes no changes in the user's document that the user has not specifically directed it to make. What it does provide is a convenient means for manipulating the text that the user types in. A computer that constantly displays the current draft on a TV screen and allows one to delete or add a paragraph in the middle or change the order of a few paragraphs or eliminate or switch words here and there with no retyping would make it possible to go through more of what we currently call drafts without the tedium and effort inevitably associated with that process in the past.

A variety of powerful text-editing systems already exist. At a minimum, these systems facilitate:

Moving around within the document by skipping over units, such as single
    characters, words, lines, sentences, paragraphs, or pages
Insertion or deletion of any quantity of text at any point in the document
Relocation or copying of a currently existing piece of text within the document
    ment
Searching for occurrences of particular entries in the document and executing various actions conditional on what is found (e.g., replacing all occurrences of ''dun'' with ''done,'' or reporting the number of

times the word "very" was used within two pages of the current location)
Saving drafts and their past histories for easy recall (protecting the user
from losing text by error and providing a step-by-step picture of the
development of a piece of writing)

The best editing systems provide all of the standard features of text
editors in a real-time "what-you-see-is-what-you-get" system. As a writer
makes changes in his document, he sees on a TV screen exactly what he is
doing and what the result is. He can specify format for his document and
can see the structuring effects this gives his work. He can see the effect of
underlining or bold face for emphasis.

In addition, numerous special aids can be added to such a system.
The spelling correction system in use at BBN is a convenient and powerful
spelling aid that can be invoked at the choice of the user. When requested,
it runs through a document, looks up every word in its dictionary, queries
the user about questionable spellings or unknown words (e.g., names),
and offers to replace misspelled words. One can also envision a computerized thesaurus that, when requested, offers alternative vocabulary for a
word that the user has indicated. It is reasonable to assume that the deaf
person, like the hearing person, has a higher recognition vocabulary than
production vocabulary and that he can therefore make use of the offerings of a thesaurus for introducing color and variety into his written
work, with the expected result that his production vocabulary will be expanded in the process.

By diminishing the penalty for typographical errors and ensuring
that changes are always easy to make, a computer text editor encourages
faster typing, and cuts the time required for polishing a document. One
can learn to ignore the imperfections of a first draft when the pain of con-
verting it to a more satisfying draft is low. Faster typing and reduced
worry about choice of words or order of presentation of ideas in the first
draft can allow a writer to record his ideas more closely in step with the
way he thinks, thereby allowing ideas to flow more naturally.

Ease in editing has advantages not only for the private preparation of
a draft, but, when desired, allows for easy utilization of editorial help. In
particular, it allows the production of a written composition — typically a
one-way language effort — to become interactive. Teachers can help a
student improve current works, rather than merely hoping that their comments and criticisms help the production of the next composition. This effectively allows both the student and teacher to avoid defining pieces of

writing as "good" or "bad" and instead to think of them as "finished" or "unfinished."

The computer editor allows the child to engage in a kind of dialogue with himself as he looks at his written ideas, adds to them, embellishes them, and takes pride in an attractively typed, personally designed as well as personally written creation. The child gains a kind of control of language that contrasts sharply with the response-to-teacher mode that is more common. The child also gains an opportunity to become active rather than passive in the business of refining his use of English.

In a project conducted at The Learning Center for Deaf Children by Richard Rubinstein of BBN, the computer system was designed to permit children and teachers to send electronic mail to each other. The computer kept copies of all messages sent or received by students. Great care has been taken to preserve privacy in this recording process and, for the protection of the interests of the children and staff at the school, all identifying information is eliminated from the record.

Here are several examples of messages sent by children at the school. The selection is reasonably representative, but these few examples cannot hope to show the full range of the children's writings and creativity. In the letters that follow, the lines beginning with "To:" and "From:" are formatted by the computer, only the names are supplied by the child.

Letters 1 through 4 are from a 15-year-old deaf girl:

Letter: 1   04-Nov-77 10:54 AM
To: (Girl 3)   From: (Jan)
      How are you? I am fine. (Girl 13) don't like you! I will sleep over (Girl 13)s house.

Letter: 2   04-Nov-77 11:03 AM
To: (Boy 9)   From: (Jan)
      Why you broken new my necklace.
      I don't like you broken new my necklace!

Letter: 3   05-Dec-77 12:17 PM
To: (Teacher 2)   From: (Jan)
      Dear (Teacher 2's last name),
      Hi! How are you? I am fine. Do you think all right (Girl 19) and me will sleep over your house. I never visit you house. Do you like lots of animals? I love gerbils, dogs mices. That's all. Do you have any dogs or cats? I know your favorite animals!!! Do you like downstair? I don's like downstair. I like to upstair. I want you go upstair again!!! Your son (name) is cute!!! Your wife's name? I don't know your wife. I think your wife and son are nice!! You are nice too!!!!!!! Where was you born? I was in (town), Ma. I live in (town). I know you live in (town) (Teacher 7) live there.

Letter: 4   03-Jan-78 12:12 PM
To: (Girl 13)   From: (Jan)
HI (Girl 13),
        WHY YOU DON'T WANT TO GO SWIMMING. I LIKE TO GO TO
SWIMMING.
DO YOU LIKE (Girl 4)? DO YOU LIKE (Girl 3)?
I LIKE YOU MUCH!!!
DO YOU WANT TO SLEEP OVER MY HOUSE? I WANT TO SEE
YOUR DOG.
I SAID "HI" YOUR MOTHER AND FAMILY. I LIKE TO YOUR
FAMILY.
YOU ARE CRAZY!!!!! HA HA HA HA HA HA HA HA HA
HA!!!!!!!!!!!!!!!!!

Letters 5 and 6 are a correspondence between two 12-year-olds:

Letter: 5   23-Nov-77 10:27 AM
To: (Boy 29)   From: (Girl 12)
HI (Boy 29),
YOU ARE VERY CUTE.
YOU ARE VERY CRAZY.
        LOVE (Girl 12)

Letter: 6   29-Nov-77 11:22 AM
To: (Girl 12)   From: (Boy 29)
Dear (Girl 12)
        You are beautiful!!!! Why cute me? Why crazy me? Bowling to come yes
or no? Do you want to go and get ice cream yes or no? I want to go to your
house.
                        love
                    (Boy 29)

Letter 7 is a social letter:

Letter: 7   05-Dec-77-08:59 AM
To: (Teacher 3)   From: (Girl 3)
        Hi! I was happy to get your ietter. I don't understand what succeeding
mean. The answer your questoin are I want to goto The (name) high school.
and yes, I like the teacher upstairs. I don't have a boyfriend. I think (Girl 32)
want to write to you. I think she want to know your address. (Boy 26) said
you are handsome. I think you are cute. Piease write to me. love, (Girl 3)

        During the first three months, "over 600 letters were sent by a group
of children who typically wrote little when given an assignment and almost nothing spontaneously" (Rubinstein and Goldenberg, 1978, p. 136).
Many of the messages were quite long.
        Jan, a 15-year-old deaf girl, was a particularly active writer. A for-
mal analysis is not needed to observe the changes in structure, style, and
volume between Letters 1 or 2 and Letter 3, which was written a month

later. Letter 4, written in a particularly silly mood and to a child, is evidence that the improvement seen in Letter 3 is not due solely to the fact that it was addressed to a teacher. Jan writes more and asks questions that expect a response, rather than the ritualized "How are you?" of Letter 1 and the rhetorical "Why you broken new my necklace" of Letter 2. She also "plays" with her English much more by using wild (and good) punctuation and more casual and varied constructions (Rubinstein and Goldenberg, 1978).

This pattern continued. At the end of February she sent a letter saying:

> Why dont you wrtie me back? Would you be happy if you slept over my house, in the spring time. Please write back soon!!!!!!!!!!!!!!!!!!!!!!!! !!!!!!!!!!!!!!!!!!!!!!!!!

Not all of the freedom and syntactic correctness she shows in this letter is permanent with her yet, as can be seen in an early April letter she addressed to me.

> Hi Paul   I cant go to wedding on April 9. But my mother said no. I want to go to weddingand (Girl 4) and me. (Girl 4) can go to wedding. But Icant go. I will try to my mother. Have nice a wedding!

What remains throughout, however, is the strongly communicative element and the fact of her expressing that in written English. The formatting games she played with her name, e.g., typing it diagonally across the page at the end of her letters, are not shown in these samples.

This genuine concern for communication is well illustrated by Girl 29's statement "I don't understand what succeeding mean" (letter 7) and Boy 29's response to Girl 12 (Letter 6). In addition, both letters show the vitality that is so obvious in all of the letters.

Composing on a Computer

The writings shown above were composed without any facilities for editing other than the ability to erase the last character or word typed on the current line. Once a carriage-return was typed to the computer, no further changes could be made to that line. This greater use of written English is valuable practice despite the uncorrected errors. Supporting this view is the observation of the teachers at The Learning Center for Deaf Children who were involved in the BBN project. They reported that several of the children (in particular, Girl 3 and Jan) have shown stunning recent improvements in their writing. It is not possible, at present, to know how much of this improvement is due directly to their loving computer mail and how much is due, for instance, to a greater sense of personal investment during English class resulting from their writing experience, but the progress is suggestive.

Although this system gave essentially no feedback on the children's language and provided extremely limited opportunities for them to edit their own letters (either at the suggestion of some reader or spontaneously), there were obvious benefits for these children. Computer mail, for the first time, offered them reliable and quick communicative contact with a person separated from them. Providing both the feedback and the editing capabilities should vastly increase the value of the system as an aid to written English acquisition.

For many deaf students, English has always been associated with pain and failure. Both the initial effort that must be expended and the amount of editing and correcting that a prelingually deaf person must go through are likely to be greater than that required of the average hearing person. That makes the efficiencies of computer editors all the more valuable to the deaf writer. Furthermore, special programs can be designed specifically for the deaf user. A limited syntactic advisor can be designed for use by a child who is capable of producing good deaf English (DE). The fact that there is some consistency in the deaf child's deviations from standard English (SE) — that deaf English might qualify as a distinct dialect (Charrow, 1974) — means that it is possible to write computer programs that can parse deaf English (in restricted contexts) and can offer the deaf child help in translating to SE. This is difficult for a computer to do in the general case, but for certain frequently occurring constructions in limited domains it can be of some help.

It is important, of course, that all of the nonpassive aids (advisors rather than mere facilitators), such as the computerized spelling corrector and thesaurus, do nothing unless invoked by the student. They should not supervise, criticize, or otherwise meddle with the student's work except when the student explicitly requests help.

Word processing systems have become commonplace in business settings and have vastly reduced the effort and personal cost in composing a satisfying document. Yet, these systems, which are entirely within the capabilities of many of the computers currently being used in schools, have not been provided for children. Such an addition to the mail system would allow students to alter their composition in any way, from minor typing corrections to full-scale structural revisions, before exposing their writing to the possibly critical eyes of a reader.

Word processing systems for the deaf may serve as a lifelong communication aid. To see the need for them, one has to imagine oneself deaf and trying to arrange a dinner party of deaf friends. Mail is slow, and if one is trying to arrange a mutually agreeable time, several mailings may be required. One can visit the others and talk in person, but people are not always home when you want them and, again, long and repeated efforts are required. Teletyping the message over telephone lines, of course, will work, but teletyping is vastly inferior to spoken conversations because it is slow and long distance charges mount up quickly. Were one a subscriber to a computer network system and able to compose and edit a message, one could send the message to all of those invited guests who also subscribe to the system. A pilot system of this sort was developed at BBN (Grignetti et al., 1977; Cerf, 1978) and a nationwide computer-based telecommunication network is currently under development at SRI, International (Harrenstien, personal communication). Current technology makes it possible for the deaf person to type his message in at one end and have it spoken at the other end, allowing a message to be sent to a hearing person without a teletype, for example, to a supermarket. Unfortunately, there is not yet an equally good technology for making the reverse translation.

Interactive Language Game

The way in which a computer text editor supports my philosophy of education of the deaf, and my understanding of the recommendations of Brennan (1975) and Wilbur (1977), should be clear. However, editors are not enough. A computer-based writing laboratory must be a rich environment. Highly exciting interactive games that parse and respond to moderately complex written commands already exist[13] and can be augmented to respond intelligently to deaf English as well as standard English. Such a game can be easily modified to understand a child regardless of defects in his English and to respond with standard English that the child can understand. This modified game would provide another use for interactive written English in context. Activities of this kind, which communicate with English rather than drill its forms, will ultimately be the most productive uses for the computer in developing language experiences for deaf children.

Many computer games involve the player in reading considerable English, and some even require answers to be written in English, rather than

---

[13]One such game is DUNGEON, created at the Programming Technology Division of the Massachusetts Institute of Technology Laboratory for Computer Science by Tim Anderston, Marc Blank, Bruce Daniels, and Dave Lebling. It was inspired by the ADVENTURE game of Crowther and Woods, and by "Dungeons and Dragons" by Gygax and Arneson. This particular game makes use of a particularly unsophisticated parser compared with others developed by some of the aforementioned.

requiring special codes or numbers. Simple parsers have been designed that, within a limited set of expectations and with a small vocabulary, simulate remarkable understanding of a considerable range of English sentences. This allows the creation of language games where the player is not restricted to responding to the computer's questions, but can initiate a communication as well. The sense of exploration and adventure in one such game, Dungeon, is very great and has engaged 12-year-olds (and 30-year-olds) at our offices for many hours at a time. The player is plunked in an imaginary magical land and is free to explore its mysteries, looking for treasures, and avoiding the dangers that lurk there. Because the player is also exploring ways of communicating with the machine, a great deal of interactive language is being used. The rather long transcript that follows (adapted from the 4/12/78 edition of the game) was created to illustrate the range of the interactive language of which the game is capable. The text of this version was designed for adult speakers of standard English. Before presenting this game transcript, it should be stressed that this implementation of the game uses a highly unsophisticated parser, one that is totally insensitive, for example, to the difference between "Walk up the staircase" and "Walk up staircase." To accommodate a different kind of user, this could be changed so that the program would understand those two sentences equally well, but would sense the difference and be able to use that information for response or language analysis statistics. In the following sample protocol, the human player's statements are indicated in boldface type.

> **Look around.**
You are in an open field west of a big white house, with a boarded front door. There is a small mailbox here.

> **Look in the mailbox.**
The mailbox is closed.

> **Open it, please.**
Opening the mailbox reveals a leaflet.

> **Read it.**
How can I read a mailbox?

> **Read the leaflet.**
Taken.

WELCOME TO DUNGEON
DUNGEON is a game of adventure, danger, and low cunning. In it you will explore some of the most amazing territory ever seen by mortal man. Hardened adventurers have run screaming from the terrors contained within!
In DUNGEON the intrepid explorer delves into the forgotten secrets of a lost labyrinth deep in the bowels of the earth, searching for vast treasures long

hidden from prying eyes, treasures guarded by fearsome monsters and dia-
bolical traps!

> **Close it.**
You must tell me how to do that to a leaflet.

> **Close the mailbox.**
Closed.

> **I like to be neat.**
I am glad you like to be neat.

> **Walk east.**
You can't walk east. The door is locked, and there is evidently no key.

> **Open the door.**
The door cannot be opened.

> **Break it.**
With what?

> **With your hands.**
Beating on a door is not very interesting.

> **Walk north.**
You are facing the north side of a white house. There is no door here, and all
the windows are barred.

> **Walk east.**
You are behind the white house. In one corner of the house there is a small
window which is slightly ajar.

> **Open the window.**
With great effort, you open the window far enough to allow entry.

> **Climb in.**
You are in the kitchen of the white house. A table seems to have been used recently for the preparation of food. A passage leads to the west and a dark
staircase can be seen leading upward. To the east is a small window which is
open. On the table is an elongated brown sack, smelling of hot peppers. A
bottle is sitting on the table. The glass bottle contains: A quantity of water

> **Pour the water on the brown sack.**
I can't make sense out of that.

> **Take the sack and the bottle.**
Brown sack: taken.
Glass bottle: taken.

> **Climb out the window.**
You are behind the white house. In one corner of the house there is a small
window which is open.

> **Walk south.**
You are facing the south side of a white house. There is no door here, and all
the windows are barred.

> **Go back.**

He who puts his hand to the plow and looks back is not fit for the kingdom of winners. What do you mean "Go back"?

> **Go norht.**

Did you mean to say "Go north"?

> **Yes**

You can't go north. The windows are all barred.

> **Go east.**

You are behind the white house. In one corner of the house there is a small window which is open.

> **Climb in.**

You are in the kitchen of the white house. A table seems to have been used recently for the preparation of food. A passage leads to the west and a dark staircase can be seen leading upward. To the east is a small window which is open.

> **Walk up staircase.**

It is pitch black. You are likely to be eaten by a grue.

> **Walk down.**

You are in the kitchen.

> **Walk west.**

You are in the living room. There is a door to the east, a wooden door with strange gothic lettering to the west, which appears to be nailed shut, and a large oriental rug in the center of the room. There is a trophy case here. A battery-powered brass lantern is on the trophy case. There is an issue of US NEWS & DUNGEON REPORT dated 4/12/78 here. On hooks above the mantelpiece hangs an elvish sword of great antiquity.

> **Take sword, lantern and report.**

Sword: taken.
Lamp: taken.
Newspaper: taken.

> **Open trophy case.**

Opened.

> **Look in case.**

The trophy case is empty.

> **Close it.**

Closed.

> **Walk east.**

You are in the kitchen.

> **Walk up stairs.**

It is pitch black. You are likely to be eaten by a grue.

> **Turn on lamp.**

The lamp is now on. You are in the attic. The only exit is stairs that lead down. There is a square brick here which feels like clay. A large coil of rope is lying in the corner. On a table is a nasty-looking knife.

>**Take everything.**
Knife: taken.
Rope: taken.
Brick: taken.

>**Go down.**
You are in the kitchen.

>**Turn off light.**
The lamp is now off.

>**Go west.**
You are in the living room. There is a door to the east, a wooden door with strange gothic lettering to the west, which appears to be nailed shut, and a large oriental rug in the center of the room. There is a trophy case here.

>**Take oriental rug.**
The rug is extremely heavy and cannot be carried.

>**Go west.**
The door is nailed shut.

>**Open it.**
The door cannot be opened.

>**Pull out the nails with the knife.**
I don't know the word OUT.

>**Inventory.**
You are carrying:
   A brick
   A rope
   A knife
   A newspaper
   A lamp
   A sword
   A glass bottle with a quantity of water
   A brown sack
   A leaflet

>**Read the newspaper.**

US NEWS & DUNGEON REPORT
4/12/78   Late Dungeon Edition
US NEWS Editorials
Important: If at first you don't succeed, try, try again!

>**Take the rug.**
The rug is extremely heavy and cannot be carried.

>**Move it.**
With great effort, the rug is moved to one side of the room. With the rug moved, the dusty cover of a closed trap-door appears.

>**Open the door.**
Which door should I open?

> **The trap door.**
The door reluctantly opens to reveal a rickety staircase descending into darkness.

> **Quit**

You score is 10 out of a total of 500 points. This score gives you the rank of Beginner.

The value of this game for a child learning to communicate through written English can be enhanced by allowing many players to explore the territory together. Picture the same game with the added ability to send a message to another player (perhaps, in reality, at the other end of the school from the first player or in another school altogether) and to ask him or her for advice on avoiding some pitfall. Cooperative play increases the score of both players and encourages communication and concern that one's messages are understood.

NOVEL SOURCES OF MEANING FOR THE AUTISTIC CHILD

That the computer and the autistic child have an excellent rapport at first seems absolutely clear (Colby, 1973; Weir and Emanuel, 1976). What the future of such a relationship would be is unknown, partly because no reported work continued over a sufficiently long time, and partly because current theoretical statements about autistic children seem inadequate to explain even the short-term successes.

It might be suggested that the machine is the natural entry into the world of autistic children because they like machines better than people or even think of themselves as machines (cf. Bettelheim, 1967). This theory is untenable as research has shown that autistic children do not avoid people. Weir and Emanuel (1976) attach significance to the fact that the machine does not make demands on the child. It is tempting to conjecture that the autistic child's insistence on sameness is satisfied by the behavior of a computer, but it is difficult to see how a child who has such learning difficulties would recognize this almost from the outset. I am left wondering what fascinates him during whatever time it takes for him to realize that the computer satisfies that obsessive desire. It may be that the autistic child is aided by the fact that the computer allows for exploration and spontaneous use without requiring imitation as a part of learning how to use it. It may be, but these things simply are not known yet.

Design considerations for a system for autistic children are, however, quite clear. We must make a computer system that accepts the inputs that the child is most easily capable of producing. Its responses must be as en-

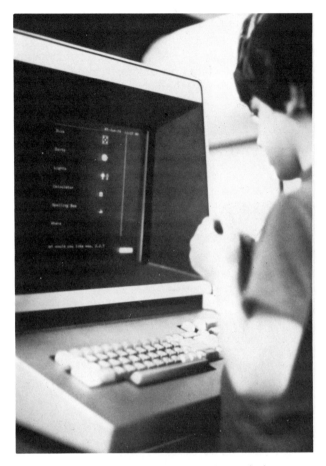

Figure 28.   Child approaching the terminal.

gaging and easily perceivable as possible. We must avoid the temptation
to "teach first," requiring that the child build some particular skill (receptive or expressive) with which he is not yet fluent and spontaneous. The
building of new skills can come later: first we must find a way for the child
to make flexible use of the skills he already has.

The computer should be receptive to all forms of input that the child
can spontaneously use. This should include typed messages and vocal
sounds. It must also be sensitive to less formal and deliberate meaningful
acts. For example, the computer should be able to sense the proximity of
the child so that a child who approaches it (see Figure 28), but is not at-

tending to it enough to touch it deliberately, can get a response. The computer should, of course, recognize direct contact (Figure 29). When we program the computer, we decide which of these input modes is most appropriate to the particular child who will use it, and how it will respond. Thus, we design the sensitivity of the machine to the capabilities and manner of each child.

The output device must be easy to attend to peripherally. A color TV screen 36 square feet in area on which one can draw in full color, for example, allows a very large effect for a very small effort.

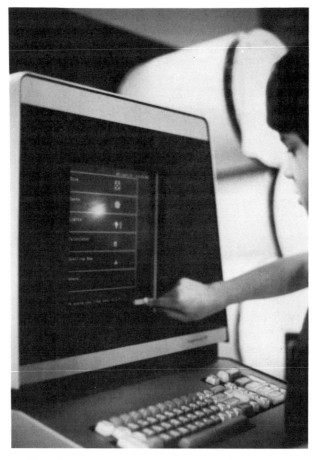

Figure 29.   Making a choice on a touch-sensitive screen.

The purposes of the variety and sensitivity of the input devices are to eliminate the need to predicate the use of the computer on the prior existence of intentional acts and to make use of stereotyped behaviors of the child. The result would be the assignment of meaning to these behaviors. Let us consider, for example, a child whose mannerisms include the typical hand-tapping on objects. Imagine that we attach some meaning to the hand-tapping by having the computer sense it and give an interesting auditory or visual feedback. Perhaps the feedback could be a "tock" from the electronic music box for each tap the child makes, or a flash on the TV screen, or, if he watches the screen closely enough, an animated cartoon that moves one step for each of his taps, or even the animation of a physical toy train. Clearly, the object of such a scheme is not to "reward" his tapping, but to take an "incommunicative" piece of behavior and endow it with meaning. I do not assume that hand-tapping is without any function or meaning to the child. That function, however, is "autistic" in the sense that it does not have a *shared* meaning or use. It is neither social nor communicative, and it is generally not specific to environmental conditions that we can recognize. Thus we are able to give the child's behavior a purpose without first requiring that the behavior be changed.

As the child becomes more interested in whatever output device is used (robot turtle, color TV, and music box), the input device must be modified to allow greater flexibility. It must become less sensitive to the child's gross movements and allow deliberate choices while the child stays near or in contact with it. The gradual narrowing of the window through which the child communicates involves a kind of behavior shaping, as uses for current behaviors are found and signs of interest appear. The important difference between this and conventional behavior modification is that the rewards are intrinsic and not contingent on the observation and approval of an outsider. Thus, the behavior shaping is not to make the child more controllable, but more controlling.

At present, it is difficult to explain the results we have seen, but we certainly have had sufficiently suggestive initial experiences to speculate about them.

The computer can be programmed to be tolerant of spelling or other errors, or it can be as literal-minded and insistent on sameness as the child is. In either case, the computer can be supremely consistent and may help establish a sense of causality for a child whose picture of the world is distorted and who has little apparent ability to effect and control. From another viewpoint, the computer's behavior is so regular that a child who has had difficulty understanding all but the most repetitive behavior of a simple toy has a chance to predict the effects of his actions in another context, and then expand his repertoire of actions and their predicted effects. He attaches meaning to his own behaviors and to the ones he teaches the computer to perform.

Both the adult teacher/therapist and the computer can be sensitive to a wide variety of behaviors that the child can produce, but, unlike a person, who is normally active, the computer is normally inert. Unlike a person, the computer does not change roles in interacting with the child. Like any mechanical object, e.g., a toaster, the computer must be "used right" if it is to do the job for which it was intended. Unlike a person, the computer cannot be assumed to be willfully insisting on a particular and arbitrary behavior (such as a spoken utterance or eye contact) before delivering the prize. There is a distinct difference between a behavior modification technique in which it is clear that the adult already knows what the child wants but withholds it until the child speaks and a machine that refuses to work until you turn it on.

It is not an established fact that an autistic child knows that difference, but it is certainly worth checking out. The behavior modification example tends to pit therapist against child in an opponent relationship, regardless of the importance of the modification. There is something to be said for using a computer, rather than a person, to simulate a machine!

By providing stimulating activities that the child can engage in without handicap, we give him a richer environment to share and to communicate about. Communicative effort is certainly motivated by these rich experiences.

Summarizing the above features of this approach, the child is put in control of a mini-world. As he is increasingly able to interact with it, it can increase its offerings, both in complexity and in scope. He can interact through it with other people, e.g., by playing a game with a teacher or even another child. The mini-world of the computer provides the constancy, regularity, availability, and on-demand stimulation without taking over or making return demands on the child. The child's motivation to do more represents taking control of this mini-world, rather than relinquishing control to an adult.

Wing (1976) has suggested that

> The brain dysfunction in autism may so reduce the child's ability to meet even the ordinary demands of everyday life that he lives in a condition of perpetual failure. This is made even worse when he is faced, in a teaching situation, with yet more tasks which are outside his specific range of abilities. So-called negativism is a predictable result. In contrast, when an autistic child is given tasks within his capacity, he is likely to be co-operative and responsive. (p. 199)

Taylor's (1976) methods of working with autistic children are

> different from those used in operant conditioning. Both approaches are structured in the sense that the teacher decides what the child should be doing, but the essence of [the games Taylor describes in her chapter] is that the child is allowed to find the rules for himself, as the normal child seems to do when acquiring language. Most operant programmes, on the other hand try to build up skills such as language by the direct teaching of every tiny step in performance. (p. 220)

Is this not reminiscent of Brennan's (1975) view of the deaf child's language learning?

Depending on the student, we may design different types of environments. Thomas liked to type words repetitively. He says each letter in a strange, tense, and tinny voice as he types it, but he never says out loud any of the words that he has typed. The computer can type each letter very beautifully and neatly on a TV screen, erase mistyped letters, say each letter with the child, and say each word out loud as the boy finishes the word with a space. If that action of the computer is intrusive, we program the computer to respond another way. If the response seems to interest the child, we keep it. Some children may enjoy and learn from the sounds of letters as they type randomly; others may want individual letters to have picture or cartoon effects. (For example, "c" draws a cat and "d" draws a dachshund.) Alternatively, the computer can type CAT and draw a beautiful cat in response to the child's verbalization "'at"; perhaps one would even want the computer to repeat the word, spoken more correctly.

If a particular child uses speech, but not yet in a regular and communicative way, the untiring and consistent responsiveness of the computer to his vocalizations may be both motivating and educational, in that the response produces a desired effect and establishes the communication value of the verbal behavior. These examples have stressed the direct relationship between the child's input and a specific language skill, but they were not intended to limit the applications to which the computer might be put. For many autistic children, nonspeech related and even nonlanguage activities might be more appropriate, especially initially.

Part IV
Research Needs

Chapter 8
Research Needs

I believe one could make a convincing argument that the amount of money that is spent attempting to solve the problems of the handicapped is so small compared to what is spent on some other things as to be a national disgrace. Consider, for example, the cost of one nuclear submarine, or that of one B1 bomber — or that of putting man on the moon. I do not want to argue against the need for a reasonable defense effort nor against a space exploration program. But it is not clear to me on what dimensions these programs are so much more important than the solution of the problems of handicapped people as to warrant such a huge disparity in the expenditure of tax dollars.[14]

Throughout this book, I have suggested research that I feel needs to be done. The purpose of this chapter is to organize that presentation.

EXPLORATIONS

Few Students, Many Contact Hours

Of the handicapped children reported in this book, the child who used the computer for the longest time spent only 12 hours with it. All of the children wanted to use it more. My experiences make me optimistic, but there is no research on the long-term benefits of computer-mediated environments. Is the excitement that we see something potentially lasting or is it primarily the natural enthusiastic greeting given to any activity that is a change of pace? This question is obviously not researchable independent of the development of good things to do with the computer. If the computer is *always* new by virtue of being the growing and flexible activity aid that I have claimed, then it will always offer a change of pace. For the device to *continue* to be novel, either the library of resources must be enormous or, far better, the user must begin to generate his own activities. This is especially true of the severely motorically handicapped person, for whom the computer is an interface to the world. Such a person must become a programmer of his or her own computer if the computer is to remain useful. We cannot expect the computer neophyte to develop all of the possibilities without our having taught him or her a large enough range of them. Specifically, we must be prepared to teach the newcomer how flexible the computer is and how to tailor it for personal use. Thus, we must develop activities that both excite and interest the rank beginner and also teach him or her how to use the computer without building a dependency on anyone else. That it is possible for even young children to learn and use a powerful computing language has been well observed in

---

[14]From a letter from R. S. Nickerson of BBN to Carl E. Sherrick, of the Psychology Department, Princeton University, April 1, 1977.

experiments with LOGO conducted at M.I.T. and elsewhere. However, specific curricula for working with any children, let alone the handicapped, have not yet been developed. One wonders what such curricula would look like.

There are people for whom the computer may only be a temporary aid to their education. Even among those who live with the computer for the rest of their lives and must become their own personal programmers, not all will be able, or want, to be programmers vocationally. In either case, we need other vocational curricula, but the disabled person's educational and experiential histories differ vastly from the norm on which standard vocational curricula are based. We must build courses that are not culturally biased against the sensorily or motorically handicapped person.

In the case of the autistic or retarded person, the beginnings have been encouraging, but there is little way of predicting how far the person and computer are capable of going together. Two possibilities are of interest. Being autistic or retarded is no guarantee against boredom, and the lives of the most severely affected of these individuals are mind-deadeningly unstimulating. Perhaps the best that an indestructible computer can offer is a sufficiently rich recreational environment to wake up the interest of those who have long faced fear, frustration, and failure. Alternatively, we may find some of these people for whom the computer offers a more natural modality for control, people who can then begin to function more normally. We have only to look at the false positive diagnoses of mental retardation — or, for that matter, to the chimpanzees and gorillas who are demolishing our casual claim that only *Homo sapiens* is capable of language — to realize how easily we can be misled by evaluations based on an inappropriate modality. Perhaps there will not be much progress to make, but we must find out.

Few Contact Hours, Many Students

Questions of the relationship of activity or language to cognition, or questions of the long-range usefulness of computers in education and therapy cannot be answered by short studies, yet short studies gain their value through the economy with which they raise important issues. Several of the physically handicapped children who used the computer had been considered retarded. Even our brief contacts raised assessments of their cognitive abilities. What about retarded children for whom we could not so easily claim that physical disabilities hindered the expression of their intellectual capability? I expect that brief excursions will continue to yield worthwhile observations for a few years. In addition to exploring new uses of the computer with these children (translate that as "newly recognized capabilities of children who have access to the computer"), we must spend some effort considering how to introduce children to it in the best way. Social designing is important, as can be seen most clearly in Annette's way of using the computer, and must not be overlooked in a misconceived zeal to individualize.

RESEARCH AND DEVELOPMENT FOR SERVICE DELIVERY

Several kinds of research that require both the educator and the engineer must be initiated. The equipment and programs I have designed and used with deaf, cerebral palsied, and cognitively impaired children are vastly inadequate for work with the blind. Talking systems have helped blind people use computers in situations where they must keep in close touch with the information that is being sent back by the computer. Electronic games, including a kind of audio Ping-Pong, have also been developed (Brugler, 1978). Verbal feedback would hardly tell much of value about TV-screen drawings, nor does it seem likely that TV drawings would have much initial salience to a blind child anyway. How must we adapt the activities, devices, and presentations to the blind or deaf-blind? In the light of several observations raised in this book, it would be interesting to work with very young deaf-blind children and to keep close track of their development.

Other computer toys for children should be developed with the idea of adapting to the child's best input or output modality. Currently, the best developed computer output devices (monochromatic and color TV, animated graphics and the physical turtle) are visually oriented. The music box and voice synthesizer are more difficult for children to play independently with and develop projects for. Anna, a language- and perception-impaired child who had been in speech therapy much of her life, enjoyed taking a turn as the speech therapist herself. When she had a chance to teach the voice synthesizer how to say things she wanted to say, she was happy to correct its pronunciation. The experience of being speech therapist was very rewarding to her for a while, but it became clear that we were ill-prepared to elaborate on the initial explorations that she had begun. Having the toys is not enough. We did not know what were really good things to do with them. At the time, we had no speech recognition equipment and therefore could not try "translation" activities as suggested in Chapter 7, but even that seems not to make full use of the play possibilities of speech synthesis.

I know of no experiments with tactile or kinesthetic output devices. What about a wheelchair that is controlled by the computer as the turtle is? What about force-feedback devices? Force-feedback control systems for cerebral palsied children might be very interesting and suggest great possibilities not only as alternate means of control but for functional habilitation as well. The three novel sources of control described in Chapter 7 have not yet been explored in the contexts I have suggested, and such research seems absolutely urgent.

The ultimate prosthetic computer for the physically handicapped person would be installed in the person's wheelchair as a part of that person's property. It must be free of wires so that the person's mobility is not limited, and it must be capable of at least text manipulation and graphics. Depending on the needs of the individual it may also have to control the movements of the wheelchair and speak out loud to enable the person to talk to others or to use the telephone. The research needed here is primarily in human factors and mechanical engineering, since the electronics of a device of the right power and size is essentially already available.

Economic arguments are hardly to the point; even at current prices, such a device with its potential for total habilitation would be cheap compared to the cost of warehousing the severely disabled person. Moreover, if each child who could benefit from such a prosthesis were to have one, economies of scale would drive the price even lower. Clever designing would produce a device that is marketable to able-bodied persons as well as to the disabled. Such is already true of the message technology that is now being developed for the deaf. That kind of mail system is far more efficient than carrying paper and is already widely used in big corporations and in government. It must inevitably become universal.

The human factors issues need considerable attention. When we design display devices for neurologically handicapped persons, we must remember that some of these persons may suffer from strobe-induced seizures. This is only the most dramatic example. I have already mentioned one of the problems with the conventional CAI model for deaf children. We must look for the more subtle problems involved in using a device during all one's waking hours or under the special circumstances that surround dependency on the device.

BASIC RESEARCH

Cognitive Development

We must take a close look at some of the questions raised about the mental development of a child who for the first time is given active control of his environment:

What does he unexpectedly know? (The experience with Jay makes it clear
that our assumptions about how people come to understand space
are not reliable.)
What common knowledge is he lacking due to experiential disadvantage?
What actual content is lost when a person has lacked the sandbox and
streetfight learning experiences?
What course does his subsequent development follow?
How much of the retardation of the autistic child is the functional result
of experiential deprivation?
Can a computer prosthesis be used by the autistic infant as soon as a diagnosis can be made in order to help that infant gain control of its environment and its perceptions?

There is much to learn that starts with the image of an infant as a
small, physically handicapped person with a meager education. Of
course, such a view is inadequate and misleading for building theories of
infant development. However, as naive as it is to consider the baby as
nothing other than a defective adult, it is equally naive to assume cognitive incapabilities where physical incapabilities are so clearly in evidence.
In the case of the defective infant, this is all the more important to remember.

It is also of vital importance that careful studies of the cognitive development of cerebral palsied and deaf-blind children be conducted. As
has already been indicated, such studies would benefit these children
directly by correcting our images of them and would shed light on some of
the most central issues of cognitive development.

Language Development

June van Lint (1975) has described the difficulties she found in communicating after a brain injury that left her totally paralyzed and without
speech. She was able to blink voluntarily and her husband began to communicate with her by reciting the alphabet and using her blinks to select
letters. I found especially meaningful her observation that once people assumed they understood, they would stop spelling and she had no way to
indicate that they should continue. As a result of this, she deliberately
scrambled her syntax to make sure people could not understand what she
meant until she had spelled out all of the important parts. Even when she
had regained enough control to type, the slowness of her communication
forced her to adopt the same kind of wrecked syntax to keep the other person from anticipating the end of her communication before she had finished. That and her abbreviated spellings were often misunderstood to be
a pathological result of her brain damage.

We cannot always use the apparent language ability of the physically handicapped child as an indicator of intelligence, and, as van Lint has shown, it may not even accurately reflect the child's true *linguistic* ability. A modality must provide ease and fluency if linguistic ability is to show. We learn that fact over and over, and are faced with the successes of signing simians to remind us when we forget.

We structure our language for use, not for showing off, and it may be extremely difficult to change purposes at a moment's notice.

Research must be done to find language adaptations suitable for low-bandwidth communication modalities. Unless some of the novel control devices described in Chapter 7 are successful, Jane and others like her will never communicate efficiently with spelled English — they do not have the speed. The needed artificial language (code) is one that gives maximum output at minimum physical effort by reducing redundancy. The reduction of redundancy, however, raises the mental effort required of the user which, to be practical, must be kept within reason. Whatever language adaptation we design, its presentation via computer allows the user's input code to be translated to standard English on output.

We must explore the language development of a child who has access to a high-bandwidth communicator interface and manageable feedback in a familiar form. For Jane, such a system might include a multi-channel EMG and speech recognition interface for coded selection of synthetically spoken syllables and phonemes.

We must explore the benefits for speech training that come from finding use for one's current vocal abilities. Computers that can respond differentially to vocal productions may be very useful here.

We must investigate word-processing technology for children. Would a text-editing capability revolutionize the teaching of high-school English composition? What would it, alone, do for the education of a deaf youngster?

Social Development

A computer network system for the deaf or for the severely physically handicapped does not solve the isolation problems of these people, but it does offer broader social contacts for some people whose social environment is presently extremely restricted. The social exchange involved in computer games requires only the ability to control the computer. No other aspect of one's body is either relevant or exposed. I have observed people who are normally shy in socially exposed situations join readily in computer network games with other people they have never met. Communication with the regular players of one's favorite game is a natural step, and I know of several people who have subsequently gone to considerable effort to meet each other.

The nationwide computer-aided telecommunications network for the deaf that is currently in development might offer wonderful opportunities for this kind of social invention if access to social activities (principal among which are games) were provided along with a personal message-sending capability.

CLINICAL DEFINITIONS

Redefining Perseveration

The various examples and explanations of repetitive behavior found in Chapter 5 need further observation and refinement. It is inadequate clinical practice to explain a behavior by saying that its repetition is pathological.

Redefining Readiness

An interesting result of the CARIS project (Geoffrion and Bergeron, 1978) was the demonstration that

> children who are normally considered unready for reading instruction are capable of learning to read if techniques are adapted accordingly. Specifically, CARIS assumes no prior mastery of English phonology and no particular interest in books or words by the children. Are these distinct skills which must be mastered before a child can learn to read, or are these limitations merely artifacts of our instructional technology? (pp. 12–13)

Redefining Assessment

Here, too, Geoffrion and Bergeron (1978) raise an interesting issue regarding assessment.

> Traditional approaches to testing are based on the assumption that the child is interested in bothering to answer questions on problems posed by the examiner. This assumption is very questionable when testing is undertaken with communication handicapped children. Exploratory learning systems provide an environment wherein the child is more easily induced to demonstrate his or her cognitive skills. One of the universal findings among projects like CARIS is that handicapped children often perform far beyond what others had thought them possible of doing. Might such systems then be a better indicator of a handicapped child's potential? (p. 13)

It is clear that a child's performance on language measures may not even be a good indicator if the child fully wants to cooperate. There is a serious need for assessment of process rather than prior achievement. I think that using the computer as I have described throughout this book provides an excellent instrument for assessing learning in process.

Redefining Active

Is control, independent of direct sensorimotor experience, enough for cognitive growth? That is, if a child cannot move a block with his hands, but can move it reliably with instructions from his voice, will that control substitute for sensorimotor experience? Does the age at which this control is experienced influence its value?

NEW COLLEAGUES

To exploit the power of this technology for assessment and teaching, we must find ways of educating professionals and handicapped individuals in its nature, potential, and use. They should be educated not to become mere consumers of the product, but to be active contributors to the development process.

TEACHING TOWARD STRENGTHS

There is probably no assumption that I rely on more in this writing than that one should teach toward a person's strengths and worry less about the weaknesses. Of course, that assumption is controversial. I cannot imagine it being resolved by research unless the value and theory components are carefully separated (see the end of Chapter 3 for one example of such a separation). Still, computer prostheses provide us with a unique opportunity to teach toward strengths in children whose strengths are usually buried behind their weaknesses. We may get some suggestive evidence of the power of teaching toward strengths by working with these children in this way.

DEMOGRAPHIC STUDIES

Current estimates put the prevalence of cerebral palsy at approximately 750,000 persons with an incidence rate of approximately 5 per 1,000 births, but the absence of any meaningful quantification of the severity of the handicapping conditions related to cerebral palsy prevents us from getting a clear picture of the total handicap. Information about the severity (loss of function) is similarly lacking about other physical disabilities. Without this information, it is difficult to establish consistent policies concerning research and service issues in this area.

Current classification systems record type (e.g., spastic, athetoid, mixed) and location (e.g., hemiplegia, paraplegia) of motor involvement, but a label such as "spastic/athetoid quadriplegic" does not tell us what the person's capabilities are. Such a person may have no useful motoric functioning at all or may be able to write capably without aids. The needs of this individual are certainly related not to his diagnostic category, but to the severity of his involvement.

How serious and of what kinds are the communication handicaps of cerebral palsied persons? There are no statistics on individuals who, by reason of neuromuscular handicap alone, are severely communicatively impaired. It is estimated that 60% of cerebral palsied individuals have speech problems (Bensberg and Sigelman, 1976), but again, the lack of quantification leaves us with no measure of the severity of these speech problems.

A center for demographic studies in cerebral palsy and related developmental disorders is needed. Such a center would gather data that would allow us to construct a quantified taxonomy of the various motor, sensory, intellectual, and communicative impairments associated with cerebral palsy. Being able to assess quantitatively the severity of the handicap is the first step needed to assign priorities and design programs to lessen the impact of cerebral palsy on the lives of its victims.

Important in the establishment of such a center would be the design of a comprehensive data collection instrument and an information retrieval system to facilitate studies of cerebral palsy. This would be of particular service to research that is already in progress, as it would provide a standard data base through which various researchers could comb with their individual perspectives. To make this wide use possible, the development of the collection instrument should be in consultation with established groups such as the Trace Center in Wisconsin, the Collaborative Study on Cerebral Palsy, Mental Retardation, and Other Neurological and Sensory Disorders of Infancy and Childhood, and others currently working on studies in cerebral palsy and related developmental disabilities. If such a data base were to maintain separate and identifiable records for each individual, it would facilitate longitudinal and follow-up studies.

SETTING PRIORITIES

What we research is colored by what we are interested in and what we deem technically and economically feasible. We must make it our top priority to support endeavors that are more fundamental than Band-Aids and that are aimed at providing people with full and rich lives. Projects that dare to be simultaneously at the frontiers of psychology, education, medicine, rehabilitation, and technology are difficult to undertake, but ultimately offer the greatest chance for achieving this goal.

Appendix

Two Videotape Transcriptions

PETER

In the following conversations, Peter does not vocalize except as noted. I have chosen not to translate his communications into English but rather to record the language he uses as directly as I can. Were he speaking French, this would be an easy matter and would require little or no explanation, except perhaps regarding my choice to do so. In fact, that choice is in the hopes of preserving the data that would be lost if the length and timing of his expressions were not kept intact. However, this language, unlike French, does not have a conventional written notation and so I must establish some conventions here. First of all, there are problems regarding which deliberately communicative movements to call signs: although I might not feel constrained to include pitch level, stress, and facial expressions were I transcribing a French statement, it is more difficult to ignore the analogous features of a signed communication. At the same time, it is thoroughly impossible — and, as this is not a study in linguistics, clearly unnecessary — to record in print all of the pauses, emphases, directions of a pointed finger, and dysfluencies. The result is that although Peter's sign language is clear and unambiguous on videotape, I have added words (in parentheses) occasionally to make the transcriptions comprehensible. It is also difficult at times to decide whether some important and communicative action that, for example, illustrates a previous statement should be considered a linguistic production and, as is occasionally possible, glossed as signs, or whether it should be described as any nonverbal behavior might be. I have made these choices with considerable thought and feeling, but not without the certain knowledge that I am imposing the structure, and not merely reporting it. Ellen speaks as she signs to Peter, but since Peter receives the signs and not the speech, I have recorded Ellen's communications in their signed form. Where her signing and speaking interact significantly, perhaps affecting her signing, mention is made of that fact.

Where (is the) Stop (button)? Where? Peter knows how to make the turtle go forward, but wonders how to tell it when to stop. He does not yet really understand that one specifies the distance forward when one makes the command. His signing is deliberate and, unlike Phillip, he watches carefully throughout even some of the longer answers.

Can't. Ellen indicates that one cannot stop the turtle once it is moving.

Peter points alternately to two buttons on the console as if continuing his question, "What about either of these?" Ellen touches his arm to draw his attention back to her.

If you want turtle move, turtle-place-here, another-place, distance-in-between, have-to tell turtle...

With animation and apparent interest, Peter anticipates the end of her sentence, signing *Turtle stop!* while she continues with *...to move forward...*

Peter finishes his command by looking and pointing at the turtle. The total effect of his command has now become "Turtle! You stop!" Ellen pauses until he looks back.

...right number. Can't just stop in between. Have-to tell turtle right number.

0.45 minutes: Peter looks back at the console, but does not move to it quickly. Although not much time is allowed for possible attempts he might make, his expression says he does not quite know what to do with it yet. Ellen decides to make it easier for Peter to control the turtle by eliminating the constant need to specify numbers, a point that Peter does not seem to understand well at the moment. Ellen signals that she wants to do something at the console and Peter moves aside to watch. Peter is very attentive as Ellen types several instructions to the computer. Once he glances at the turtle to see if it is doing anything, but otherwise he focuses on Ellen and the console, which is now typing back to them. Ellen has read in a program that allows Peter to control forward and backward motion as well as right and left turning with only the letters F, B, R, and L. She tells him that there is a new program and explains that it wants him to type his name. He types his name and looks back at her for more instructions. (1.75 minutes)

Now. Only have-to say F, B, R, or L. She shows him a prepared chart, pointing to the Forward, Backward, Right, and Left on the chart and then re-explains, pointing to each line and signing the effect. *Forward, Backward, Turn-right, Turn-left. OK? Just one letter now.*

Throughout both of these explanations, Peter has maintained his attention, nodding occasionally to indicate that he comprehends. When Ellen has finished her list of the new commands, he asks if there is not, perhaps, one more.

Stop?

Before Ellen begins to sign her response, her expression has answered him
"no," so that Peter is already signing *Can't, can't* as Ellen continues

Don't-have-to use stop.

Peter is not yet used to the new way of doing things. Earlier, he had to type
out a full command, such as FD 100, and then end the line with the green button to produce an effect. He often would try to stop the turtle in the middle of
some action by hitting the red stop button. He hesitates, and Ellen begins to
explain again.

This-word-on-list, F make turtle go forward

Peter checks his understanding.

*(This) F (here in typewriter makes), that (turtle go forward). (But if I push
this button, it) stop!* Ellen shakes her head "no," but Peter continues his
query. *Red, that-one, red?* Ellen is about to answer, but her "no" was sufficient and he changes the question. *(What about that) green (button) there?*

Don't need that now. I, uh.... Look-over-there!

Ellen demonstrates moving the turtle forward while both watch.

2.7 minutes: Peter tries it. His whole manner shows strong interest
and enjoyment, but it is a picture of quiet concentration. He makes several moves with the turtle, watches it closely, and then points to a letter on
the keyboard that he had not been using and looks questioningly at Ellen.
She signed that it was not needed and he returned to using the ones he
knew worked. The turtle is in a kidney-shaped maze with a tower at the
end of it. Peter has begun to drive the turtle through somewhat swiftly
with no difficulty deciding on the correct direction for his turns. His
handling of the keyboard now has a sense of sureness about it. He may
search for a letter, but once having found it presses it with confidence and
without hesitation. Once, after he moved the turtle, he broke into a very
pleased smile, caught Ellen's eye, and signed *Smart!*.

4.1 minutes: The distance that the turtle moves with each F is fixed.
Sometimes he sees that the turtle must go a long distance and he presses F
several times in quick succession before the turtle has had a chance to respond to them all. Other times, he moves very cautiously, waiting for the
turtle to come to a complete stop before he gives it another command. Although he did not seem to understand the significance of the distance inputs to the forward command earlier, he is clearly anticipating the
amounts of forward commands to give and not driving solely from constant feedback. This may have been his best chance to experiment with
numerical predictions. He often stops and twirls his finger in the direction

he wishes to turn the turtle and then finds the letter that turns the turtle that way.

4.9 minutes: (Tape unclear) *Turn, turn, turn....* He points to the turtle and looks at Ellen. *Small (turn).* Ellen shows she feels it needs a turn, and then he signs *Dunno!* (conversation between Peter and Ellen — tape is clear, but their conversation is not) The object is to knock over the tower. He adjusts his aim, grins widely, and signs.

(I) Think (that's it.) His F is an unusually confident and forceful, F, and indeed his aim was correct. He expected it to knock the tower over, but the turtle just barely reached the tower on that move. She he gave it another F. This time it hit the tower, but it only moved the tower a bit and didn't knock it over. He pushes several Fs in rapid succession and then gets the idea of shoving the tower over the edge of the table. He has to be careful, of course, not to drive the turtle off the edge at the same time. As Ellen gets up to stop him from driving it too far, he signs *(I'm being) Careful, careful! Almost, almost almost (at the edge)!* He turns the turtle a bit to gently nudge the tower off the edge, but Ellen goes to protect the turtle anyway. He knows the next move will do it, and strikes the command with a flourish! The tower crashes, and he looks as pleased as can be.

6.6 minutes: Pause, he assumes a pensive look with his finger to his mouth in the gesture we associate with "Shh!" and then *Idea!!!* He scrapes all of the blocks back into the barrel, and then removes a few to set up a road for the turtle. There is a gap in the tape here and we do not know how long he has spent building the one road, but he discovers that the road had to be debugged, as it was not wide enough for the turtle. When the tape starts again, he has already begun rebuilding the road, but this time with the turtle already in it. Total 8.7 minutes elapsed.

PHILLIP

Phillip has set up a large open square of wooden blocks on a table and has built a single wall of blocks from the midpoint of one side into the middle of the square dividing the territory into a U-shaped maze for the turtle. He sets the turtle facing north in the left side and plans to drive it to the other side. His plan is to back the turtle down the left side of the U, turn the turtle to the right, drive it forward along the bottom until it clears the center wall, and then turn it left again to drive it forward up the right side of the U. The following narrative is marked off in minute-long paragraphs to give some indication of the length of time involved in his work. Before the videotape was started he had already been working for some time, probably about 15 minutes.

The first minute: Phillip types the command BK (to BACK the turtle up) and then mistypes the distance. He signs *wrong! five, oh, five, oh,* looks at Ellen for a moment and then back down at his console. He beckons *come here* with crooked finger and then repeats *wrong! wrong! (pause) 55* indicating the change he had wanted, 50 instead of 55. Ellen types the rubout. He returns to his typing and even though he is not looking, she signs *that's enough.* Phillip signs *nuts!* and looks back at Ellen. She begins signing *if you give more,* but he looks away after her *if.* She pauses and then signs *yes* even though he is still not looking. He ends the line, signs *fine* to himself, looks up as the turtle backs up and signs *I won!* He types the next command. Phillip's vision is not very good and he cannot see the turtle well enough from where he sits, so he must either watch Ellen as she indicates the direction (heading) and sometimes the position of the turtle, or get up from his console and walk over to the turtle to look at it more closely. This time he chooses to see for himself. He signs and chirps *almost!* and lok to Ellen. He indicates the next move the turtle must make. His *right rotation* sign is a large spatial gesture, a mime of holding the turtle between his two slightly curved palms and rotating it. He seems to be thinking out loud rather than intending any communication with Ellen or me. He smiles broadly, gives a single solid clap, glances at Ellen, and returns to the console. He turns the turtle to the right and looks up to watch the turtle as it turns. He checks with Ellen, who indicates the turtle's current heading. He turns the turtle again, watching as it obeys.

The second minute: He looks at Ellen, who again is pointing the turtle's heading, looks at the turtle, looks back at Ellen again, and then gets up to investigate the matter himself. The turtle was not backed up far enough to clear the wooden cube at the end of the middle wall before he made it face right, so he removes the cube. Then he slides the next block, a wedge, toward the turtle (parallel to the direction the turtle is facing) to see if the turtle will clear it. The turtle will easily pass with room left over, so he moves the wedge back toward, but not quite to, its original position. He toys with the idea of placing the cube behind the wedge (nearer the turtle) and extending beyond the end of the wedge to make the passage for the turtle somewhat narrower, but decides to remove the cube altogether. *Fine,* he signs. He commands the turtle FORWARD, looks up, and says something to the turtle (maybe "go!"?), but does not sign. Ellen wants to show him something. His movements are so animated, he gets up with lively hop and skips over to Ellen and the turtle. She picks up the turtle to show him the trace that it has left underneath it. He chirps excitedly, waving an extended hand near the trace the turtle had made as it backed down the left side of the U. Although the tone is clearly excitement, it is not clear what exactly his chirp meant. He leans over the table to watch as Ellen measures off with her hand the distance that the turtle has just travelled along the bottom of the U. She copies that distance twice more to show where the turtle would be two similar FORWARDs from now. Before she has even completed her second step, he has understood how to estimate the measurements he needs, made his "aha!" clap, and skipped back to the console.

The third minute: Ellen is still replacing the turtle as he begins typing. She follows him over to the console and watches as he types his next FORWARD. He fixes his eyes on the turtle as it obeys, gives one long chirped "Oh!!" He shows no indication of mouthing any particular word, but signs *forward* several times, bouncing his knee excitedly and looking up at Ellen with a very pleased smile. His "oh" evolves into an "oo" as he makes the informal sign meaning *not quite*. This time, feeling the need for a much tinier adjustment, his FORWARD is shorter than the last two. He looks at the turtle, then soberly to Ellen signing *one more?* and saying it with a clear and fully appropriate "What do you think?" inflection. She barely nods and he repeats the command for the turtle to go FORWARD a very short distance. Without looking at Ellen, he spontaneously signs *fine fine*. He gets up to inspect closely and adjusts the wedge to put it back to where it had been before his last adjustment moved it slightly out of line. As he skips back to his chair he makes the "raspberry" sound and signs *dummy*. He is about to type again, but pauses, looks up at the turtle, and plans out its next movements in the air. Although his signing spatially represents the turtle, he does not follow the order of moves the turtle must make to achieve his goal. First his thumb signs *other*, meaning that the next turn must be the "other way," that is, a left rotation. Then he indicates the new direction that the turtle will move in. Finally, he signs *left rotation*. Ellen asks *which way* and Phillip looks over his shoulder at the chart that shows what computer word translates "left rotation." He sees LT (the abbreviation for LEFT TURN), and looks back. Ellen copies his *left rotation* sign as he begins to spell LT, LT watching her closely apparently to check to see if he is correct. He verbalizes what sounds like the "el" of "el tee."

The fourth minute: He rotates the turtle left once about 45°, looks at it, rotates it some more, again about the same amount, looks, signs the direction it should go, and then gets up to inspect. Using his slide-the-block technique he sees that the turtle may scrape the center wall if it were to go straight in as he has aimed it. He backs into his chair signing *fine fine* with his left hand and then *almost*. FORWARD. He gets up to check on the wall. Turtle is, indeed, very close and he makes slight adjustments to the wall.

The fifth minute: Ellen signs *You can move the turtle* and continues by showing a slight zigzag that takes the turtle farther away from the center wall. He plans out the path with his hands and then backs up to his seat. The telephone lines have been giving us trouble by sending garbage to the computer that the computer interprets as the panic stop command. The effect is harmless, but causes Phillip's console to print STOPPED! each time this happens. Phillip saw five or six of them at his console when he returned and, chirping a threat, looked to Ellen for help while shaking his fist at the console in mock anger. It had happened earlier and he knew that the consequences were not serious, but still he was not sure what should be done. Ellen typed a space, signed *OK*, and he continued. He rotated the turtle a bit to the right and began to type a forward command. He intended FORWARD 50, but typed 59 by mistake, and with a little stamp, he signed and crowed a very lively *wrong, five nine, five nine, wrong.* He corrected his error, signed a crisp, one-handed *exact* and then, sotto voce (so to speak) *mistake,* his whole demeanor saying "hmmph! mistake, indeed." He watched as the newly corrected FORWARD 50 was executed, leaned slightly toward the turtle, and gave it three short, deliberate claps. His expression was a humorous combination of being genuinely pleased with himself and applauding his efforts, while teasing the turtle as if to say "Congratulations, dummy, for finally figuring out which way to go!"

The sixth minute: Phillip rotated the turtle back toward the left, straightening it as he continued to park it. Again he applauded the turtle, but this time with a much smaller gesture with not a trace of sarcasm — entirely a compliment to the beautiful turn the turtle had just executed, and looking up at Ellen as he clapped. Ellen clapped a light clap, too, and walked back to the table. FORWARD. He walked up to the table himself, clapped one loud clap for the turtle, looked up at Ellen, and returned to finish the job. One more FORWARD did it. He looked up, signed a very casual one-handed *celebrate,* much like the bored "whoopie!" of someone who has just succeeded in doing something but does not want to let on that it was any work at all. His smile was the giveaway. With a little, cocky, oh-it-was-nothing shake of the head, he turned back to the console. There was nothing else to do, so he got up, removed the middle wall, and changed the problem. He signed several moves that the turtle might make, but was again thinking out loud rather than trying to communicate. No clear goal was really established this time. He pointed to the pen in the turtle, showed *up* with his thumb, returned to the seat and spelled

PU, PU, correct! while verbalizing "pen up." He typed PU and watched the result. It was the first time that he had given that command. He was so very pleased with the result that he gave the turtle one solid clap and then shook hands with himself!

The seventh minute: He pulled himself up straight in his chair and as he tossed his head slightly back, he made a gracefully florid gesture upward with an upturned palm, beckoning the pen to move up with a princely signed command! His pride was crowned as he placed his hands on his hips to show how easy it had been. What power! Movement at his command! He finished his story: *correct!, it moved up, fine, easy!* saying "pen up" as he signed *up*. He paused to think what comes next and held his mouth closed, meaning *don't tell me*. He followed that with an "oh well" shoulder shrug and then some more typing. A typographical error spurred his animated and chirped *wrong* and then after shaking a fist at himself, a somewhat more subdued *wrong,* also spoken as well as signed. He commanded the turtle to back up and before it had a chance to be executed, he ran over to the turtle, bent over it with his hands folded behind his back, and smiled upon it as it followed his order. He claps his hands once, puts a hand up in a policeman-like *stop* and hoots a pleased "oop." Exactly seven minutes.

There is a gap of unknown length in the tape here, probably on the order of 5 to 10 minutes. Phillip's interest and attention never flag, although the distractions around him are mounting. There may be as many as 20 people gathered, including the Crotched Mountain staff, other students, and "foreigners," people whom friendly Phillip has never met. He looks at the clock twice in rapid succession, perhaps knowing that we had another student scheduled soon or perhaps recalling the chewing out that a counselor had given him the day before when he stayed with us instead of going to some other event at which he had been expected. The one "distraction" that catches his attention is a mid-teenage friend who wanders in. Phillip quickly signs *come over* and has to repeat with emphasis to convince his slightly reluctant friend. *Come over! (pause), try FD.* Phillip takes his friend's hand and types the letters FD 200 with it. He hangs on to his friend's hand as the turtle moves. I could not see his typing and so asked what number he used. He let go of his friend to sign the answer *two oh oh* which he pronounced that way as he signed it. His friend retreated, but Phillip motioned him back (also saying the word "back"), grabbed him again, and typed another command with his hand. Both times the friend was amused by the turtle's response, but again he pulled away while Phillip signed *one more, one more, one more* and then gave up, and shrugged his shoulders.

References

Amato, A., Hermsmeyer, C. A., and Kleinman, K. M. 1973. Use of electromyographic feedback to increase inhibitory control of spastic muscles. Phys. Ther. 53:1063–1066.

Athey, I. Language, Reading and the Deaf. In H. Reynolds (ed.), Gallaudet College Conference on Reading in Relation to Deafness. Gallaudet College Press, Washington, D.C. (in press.)

Ault, R. L. 1977. Children's Cognitive Development: Piaget's Theory and the Process Approach. Oxford University Press, New York.

Austin, H. 1974. A computational view of the skill of juggling. AI Memo No. 330. Artificial Intelligence Laboratory of Massachusetts Institute of Technology, Cambridge.

Baker, B. 1976. Parent involvement in programming for developmentally disabled children. In L. L. Lloyd (ed.), Communication Assessment and Intervention Strategies. University Park Press, Baltimore.

Bensberg, G. J., and Sigelman, C. K. 1976. Definitions and Prevalence. In L. L. Lloyd (ed.), Communication Assessment and Intervention Strategies. University Park Press, Baltimore.

Berko, M. J. 1975. An electronic device for speech improvement in persons with cerebral palsy and related neurologically based speech impairments. Unpublished manuscript. Available from the author at 305 B Roberts Building, 1377 E. Stroop Rd., Kettering, Oh., 45429.

Best, B., and Roberts, G. C. 1975. Cognitive development in young deaf children. Research Report No. 92. Minneapolis Research, Development and Demonstration Center in Education of Handicapped Children, Minneapolis.

Bettelheim, B. 1967. The Empty Fortress. The Free Press, New York.

Boothroyd, A., Archambault, P., Adams, R. E., and Storm, R. D. 1975. Use of a computer-based system of speech training aids for deaf persons. Volta Rev. 77(3):178–193.

Brennan, M. 1975. Can deaf children acquire language? Am. Ann. Deaf 120(5):463–479.

Brill, R. G. 1974. The Education of the Deaf. Gallaudet College Press, Washington, D.C.

Brudny, J., Korein, J., Grynbaum, B. B., Friedmann, L. W., Weinstein, S., Sachs-Frankel, G., and Belandres, P. V. 1976. EMG feedback therapy: A review of treatment of 114 patients. Arch. Phys. Med. Rehabil. 57:55–61.

Brudny, J., Korein, J., Levidow, L., Grynbaum, B. B., Lieberman, A., and Friedmann, L. W. 1974. Sensory feedback therapy as a modality of treatment in central nervous system disorders of voluntary movement. Neurology 24:925–932.

169

Brugler, J. S. 1978. Microcomputer-based sensory aids for the handicapped. In J. C. Warren, Jr. (ed.), Proceedings of the 2nd West Coast Computer Faire, pp. 70–72. Computer Faire Inc., Palo Alto, Cal.

Bruner, J. 1964. The course of cognitive growth. Am. Psychol. 19:1–15.

Carrier, J. K., Jr. 1976. Application of a nonspeech language system with the severely language handicapped. In L. L. Lloyd (ed.), Communication Assessment and Intervention Strategies. University Park Press, Baltimore.

Cerf, V. 1978. The electronic mailbox: A new communication tool for the hearing impaired. Am. Ann. Deaf 123(6):768–772.

Charrow, V. 1974. Deaf English — An investigation of the written English competence of deaf adolescents. University Microfilms International, Ann Arbor.

Clark, C. R., and Woodcock, R. W. 1976. Graphic systems of communication. In L. L. Lloyd (ed.), Communication Assessment and Intervention Strategies, University Park Press, Baltimore.

COBOL instruction for the handicapped. 1976. Communications of the ACM 19(11):650.

Colby, K. 1973. Rationale for computer based treatment of language difficulties in non-speaking autistic children. J. Autism Child. Schizo. 3(3):254–260.

Colby, K. 1975. An objective measurement of nonspeaking children's performance with a computer-controlled program for the stimulation of language behavior. J. Autism Child. Schizo. 5(2):139–146.

Colby, K., and Smith, D. C. 1971. Computers in the treatment of non-speaking autistic children. In J. H. Masserman (ed.), Current Psychiatric Therapies. Grune & Stratton, New York.

Condon, W. S. 1975. Multiple response to sound in dysfunctional children. J. Autism Child. Schizo. 5(1):37–56.

Conner, L. E. 1967. Recent trends in education of the deaf. In F. McConnell and P. H. Ward (eds.), Deafness in Childhood. Vanderbilt University Press, Nashville.

Conner, L. E. 1972. That the deaf may hear and speak. Volta Rev. 74(9):518–527.

Cruickshank, W. M. (ed.) 1976. Cerebral Palsy: A Developmental Disability. 3rd Rev. Ed. Syracuse University Press, Syracuse.

Cruickshank, W. M., and Hallahan, D. P. with Bice, H. V. 1976a. The evaluation of intelligence. In W. M. Cruickshank (ed.), Cerebral Palsy: A Developmental Disability. 3rd Rev. Ed. Syracuse University Press, Syracuse.

Cruickshank, W. M., and Hallahan, D. P. with Bice, H. V. 1976b. Personality and behavioral characteristics. In W. M. Cruickshank (ed.), Cerebral Palsy: A Developmental Disability. 3rd Rev. Ed. Syracuse University Press, Syracuse.

DeMyer, M. K. 1976. Motor, perceptual-motor and intellectual disabilities of autistic children. In L. Wing (ed.), Early Childhood Autism. 2nd Ed. Pergamon Press, London.

DeMyer, M. K., Alpern, G. D., Barton, S., DeMyer, W. E., Churchill, D. W., Hingtgen, J. N., Bryson, C. Q., Pontius, W., and Kimberlin, C. 1972. Imitation in autistic, early schizophrenic and non-psychotic subnormal children. J. Autism Child. Schizo. 2(3):264–287.

Denton, D. M. 1970. Remarks in support of a system of total communication for deaf children. In Communication Symposium. Proceedings of a conference held at Maryland School for the Deaf, pp. 5–6. Frederick.

DiCarlo, L. M. 1972. They Grow in Silence: A Review. Volta Rev. 74(5):280–287.
Doubler, J. A., Childress, D. S., and Strysik, J. S. 1978. A microcomputer-based control and communication system for the severely disabled. Proceedings of the 5th Annual Conference on Systems and Devices for the Disabled, pp. 157–160, June 7–9, Houston.
Drumm, P. R. 1972. "Total communication" — Fraud or reality? Volta Rev. 74(9):564–569.
Dugdale, S., and Vogel, P. 1978. Computer-based instruction for hearing impaired children in the classroom. Am. Ann. Deaf 123(6):730–743.
Elkind, D. 1967. Piaget and Montessori. Harvard Educ. Rev. 37(4):535–545.
Elliot, L. L. 1978. Development of communication aids for the deaf. Hum. Factors 20(3):295–306.
Eulenberg, J. B. 1976. Individualization in a speech prosthesis system. Paper presented at the Conference on Systems and Devices for the Disabled, June 10–12, Tufts New England Medical Center, Boston.
Eulenberg, J. B., and Vanderheiden, G. C., 1978. We are a community. Communication Outlook 1(1):1.
Evans, R. L. 1973. Jean Piaget: The Man and his Ideas. E. P. Dutton & Co., New York.
Fant, L. 1974. Ameslan: The communication system of choice. In P. Fine (ed.), Deafness in Infancy and Early Childhood. Medcom Press, New York.
Farwell, R. M. 1976. Speech reading: A research review. Am. Ann. Deaf 121(1): 19–30.
Finley, W. W., Niman, C., Standley, J., and Ender, P. 1976. Frontal EMG-biofeedback training of athetoid cerebral palsy patients. Biofeedback Self-Regulation 1(2):169–182.
Flavell, J. H. 1977. Cognitive Development. Prentice Hall, Inc., Englewood Cliffs, N.J.
Fletcher, J. D., and Beard, M. H. 1973. Computer-assisted instruction in language arts for hearing-impaired students. Psychology and Education Series, Technical Report No. 215. Institute for Mathematical Studies in the Social Sciences, Stanford University, Stanford, Cal.
Foulds, R., and Gaddis, E. 1975. A practical application of an electronic communication device in a special needs classroom. Proceedings of Conference on Devices and Systems for the Disabled, pp. 77–81. Krusen Center for Research and Engineering, Temple University Health Sciences Center, Philadelphia.
Furth, H. 1966. Thinking Without Language. The Free Press, New York.
Furth, H. 1973. Deafness and Learning: A Psychological Approach. Wadsworth Publishing Co., Inc., Belmont, Cal.
Galbraith, G. 1978. An interactive computer system for teaching language skills to deaf children. Am. Ann. Deaf 123(6):706–711.
Geoffrion, L. D. 1977. Videotape and transcripts of sessions with C.A.R.I.S. Unpublished materials, University of New Hampshire at Durham.
Geoffrion, L. D., and Bergeron, R. D. 1978. Initial reading through computer animation. Occasional Paper No. 1, Department of Education, University of New Hampshire at Durham.
Goodenough-Trepagnier, C. 1976a. Development of a communications system for cerebral palsied children without articulate speech. Paper presented to the

Third International Scientific Conference of the International Federation of Learning Disabilities, August, Montreal.

Goodenough-Trepagnier, C. 1976b. Developpement et premiere implantation experimentale du systeme de communication pour les infirmes moteurs cerebraux sans langage parle: PAR LE SI LA B. Departement de Linguistique, Universite de Quebec a Montreal.

Goodwin, M. S., and Goodwin, T. C. 1969. In a dark mirror. Mental Hygiene 53:550–563.

Grignetti, M., Myer, T., Nickerson, R., and Rubinstein, R. 1977. Computer aided communications for the deaf. Report No. 3738. Bolt Beranek and Newman Inc., Cambridge, Mass.

Hardeman, M. (ed.). 1974. Children's Ways of Knowing — Nathan Isaacs on Education, Psychology and Piaget. Teachers College Press, New York.

Harris, F. A. 1971. Inapproprioception: A possible sensory basis for athetoid movements. Phys. Ther. 51:761–770.

Harris, F. A., Speman, F. A., and Hymer, J. W. 1972. Therapy for cerebral palsy employing artificial sense organs for alternatives to proprioceptive feedback. Proceedings of the 1972 Carnahan Conference on Electronic Prosthetics, pp. 1–4, University of Kentucky, Lexington.

Harris, F. A., Speman, F. A., and Hymer, J. W. 1974. Electronic sensory aids as treatment for cerebral palsied children. Inappropriception: Part II. Phys. Ther. 54:354–365.

Hermelin, B., and O'Connor, N. 1970. Psychological Experiments with Autistic Children. Pergamon Press, London.

Jordan, N. 1972. Is there an Achilles' heel in Piaget's theorizing? Hum. Dev. 15(6):379–382.

Kafafian, H. 1973. C/R/I Final Report: Study of Man-Machine Communications Systems for the Handicapped. Vol. III. Cybernetics Research Institute, Washington, D.C.

Kanner, L. 1943. Autistic disturbances of affective contact. Nerv. Child 2:217–250.

Kephart, N. 1971. The Slow Learner in the Classroom. 2nd Ed. Charles E. Merrill Publishing Co., Columbus.

Kleinman, K. M., Keister, M. E., Riggin, C. S., Goldman, H., and Korol, B. 1975. Use of EMG feedback to inhibit spasticity and increase active extension in stroke patients, Paper presented to the Society for Psychophysical Research, Toronto.

Kopp, C. B., and Shaperman, J. 1973. Cognitive development in the absence of object manipulation during infancy. Dev. Psychol. 9:430.

LaVoy, R. W. 1957. Ricks communicator. Except. Child 23:338–340.

Lane, H. S. 1976. The profoundly deaf: Has oral education succeeded? Volta Rev. 78(7):329–340.

Layzer, A. 1976. Computer animated and textured presentation of language for the deaf. Am. Ann. Deaf 121(1):38–43.

Lencione, R. M. 1976. The development of communication skills. In W. M. Cruickshank (ed.), Cerebral Palsy: A Developmental Disability. 3rd Rev. Ed. Syracuse University Press, Syracuse.

Lowenthal, B. 1978. Piaget's preoperational stage of development and applications for special preschoolers. In R. Weizmann, R. Brown, R. J. Levinson, and

P. A. Taylor (eds.), Piagetian Theory and the Helping Professions. Proceedings of the 7th Interdisciplinary Conference (Vol. 1), pp. 308–314. Available from Mail Order Dept., USC Bookstore, University of Southern California, Los Angeles.

Luster, M. J., and Vanderheiden, G. C. 1974. Preliminary Annotated Bibliography of Communication Aids. Trace Center, 922 ERB, University of Wisconsin, Madison.

Markowicz, H. 1972. Some sociolinguistic considerations of American Sign Language. Sign Lang. Studies 1:15–41.

Marks, N. C. 1974. Cerebral Palsied and Learning Disabled Children. Charles C Thomas Publisher, Springfield, Ill.

Marshall, N. R., and Hegrenes, J. 1972. The use of written language as a communication system for an autistic child. J. Speech Hear. Disord. 37(2):258–261.

Martin, E. 1972. Audition, Speech, and Methodology. Volta Rev. 74(9):528–529.

McDonald, E. T., and Schultz, A. R. 1973. Communication boards for cerebral-palsied children. J. Speech Hear. Disord. 38(1):73–88.

Melcer, D., and Peck, R. F. 1967. Sensori-motor experience and concept formation in early childhood — Final Report. University of Texas, Austin

Miller, A., and Miller, E. E. 1973. Cognitive-developmental training with elevated boards and sign language. J. Autism Child. Schizo. 3(1):65–85.

Mindel, E. D., and Vernon, M. 1971. They Grow in Silence: The Deaf Child and his Family. National Association of the Deaf, Silver Spring, Md.

Mira, M., and Hoffman, S. 1974. Educational programming for multihandicapped deaf-blind children. Except. Child 40:513–514.

Morse, P. A. 1974. Infant speech perception: A preliminary model and review of the literature. In R. L. Schiefelbusch and L. L. Lloyd (eds.), Language Perspectives — Acquisition, Retardation, and Intervention. University Park Press, Baltimore.

Moskowitz, B. A. 1978. The acquisition of language. Sci. Am. 239(5):92–108.

Nickerson, R. S., and Stevens, K. N. 1973. Teaching speech to the deaf: Can a computer help? IEEE Transact. Audio Electroacoust. AU-21(5):445–455.

Nickerson, R. S., Kalikow, D. N., and Stevens, K. N. 1976. Computer-aided speech training for the deaf. J. Speech Hear. Disord. 41(1):120–132.

Nye, P. W. 1972. Selected research, development and organizational needs to aid the visually impaired. Proceedings of the 1972 Carnahan Conference on Electronic Prosthetics, pp. 41–43. University of Kentucky, Lexington.

O'Brien, K. 1977. Report on first six-week period of turtle project. Unpublished internal memo. Special Education Department, B.O.C.E.S. Putnam/Northern Westchester Education Center, Walden School, Yorktown Heights, N.Y.

Papert, S. 1971a. A computer laboratory for elementary schools. Logo Memo No. 1. Artificial Intelligence Laboratory of Massachusetts Institute of Technology, Cambridge.

Papert, S. 1971b. Teaching children thinking. Logo Memo No. 2. Artificial Intelligence Laboratory of Massachusetts Institute of Technology, Cambridge.

Papert, S. 1973. Uses of technology to enhance education. Logo Memo No. 8. Artificial Intelligence Laboratory of Massachusetts Institute of Technology, Cambridge.

Piaget, J. 1937. Principal factors determining intellectual evolution from childhood to adult life. In Harvard Tercentenary Publication No. 1. Factors Determining Human Behavior, pp. 32–48. Harvard University Press, Cambridge.

Piaget, J. 1971. Science of Education and the Psychology of the Child. Viking Press, New York.

Prizant, B. 1978. An analysis of the functions of immediate echolalia in autistic children. Unpublished doctoral dissertation. State University of New York, Buffalo.

Pulaski, M. A. B. 1971. Understanding Piaget. Harper & Row Publishers, New York.

Ricks, D. M., and Wing, L. 1976. Language, communication and the use of symbols. In L. Wing (ed.), Early Childhood Autism. 2nd Ed. Pergamon Press, London.

Rimland, B. 1972. Progress in research. In AUTISM — Proceedings of the 4th Annual Meeting of the National Society for Autistic Children, pp. 21–32. Flint, Mich.

Rosen, M., and Durfee, W. 1978. Preliminary report on EYECOM, an eye movement detection and decoding system for non-vocal communication. Proceedings of the 5th Annual Conference on Systems and Devices for the Disabled. pp. 167–171, June 7–9, Houston.

Rowell, D., Dalrymple, G., and Olsen, J. 1978. UNICOM: A universal communication and control system for the non-verbal motor impaired. Proceedings of the 5th Annual Conference on Systems and Devices for the Disabled, pp. 231–234, June 7–9, Houston.

Rubinstein, R., and Goldenberg, E. P. 1978. Using a computer message system for promoting reading and writing in a school for the deaf. Proceedings of the 5th Annual Conference on Systems and Devices for the Disabled, pp. 135–138, June 7–9, Houston.

Schein, J. D., and Delk, M. T. 1974. The Deaf Population of the United States. National Association of the Deaf, Silver Spring, Md.

Scherer, P. A., Ling, D., Mindel, E. D., and Rosenstein, J. 1972. Statements of panel of reactors on oralism/auralism and "total communication." Volta Rev. 74(9):552–563.

Stokoe, W. C., Casterline, D. C., and Croneberg, C. G. 1976. A Dictionary of American Sign Language on Linguistic Principles. Linstok Press, Washington, D.C.

Suding, R. 1978. Electronics for the handicapped. In J. C. Warren, Jr. (ed.), Proceedings of the 2nd West Coast Computer Faire, p. 31. Computer Faire Inc., Palo Alto, Cal.

Suppes, P. 1971. Computer assisted instruction for deaf students. Am. Ann. Deaf 116(5):500–508.

Taylor, J. E. 1976. An approach to teaching cognitive skills underlying language development. In L. Wing (ed.), Early Childhood Autism. 2nd Ed. Pergamon Press, London.

Upton, H. 1968. Wearable eyeglass speech reading aid. Am. Ann. Deaf 113: 222–229.

U.S. Department of Health, Education and Welfare. 1976. Programs for the Handicapped. December 20, Office for Handicapped Individuals, Washington, D.C.

Vanderheiden, G. C. (ed.), 1978. Non-vocal Communication Resource Book. University Park Press, Baltimore.

Vanderheiden, G. C., and Grilley, K. (eds.), 1976. Non-vocal Communication Techniques and Aids for the Severely Physically Handicapped. University Park Press, Baltimore.

van Lint, J. 1975. My New Life. Neyenesch Printers, Inc., San Diego.

Vernon, M. 1967. Relationship of language to the thinking process. Arch. Gen. Psychiatry 16:325–333.

Vernon, M. 1968. Fifty years research. J. Rehabil. Deaf 1(4):1–12.

Vernon, M. 1969. Sociological and psychological factors associated with hearing loss. J. Speech Hear. Res. 12(3):541–563.

Vernon, M. 1970. Myths about the education of deaf children. Proceedings of a conference held at Maryland School for the Deaf, pp. 20–24. Frederick.

Vernon, M. 1971. Psychodynamics surrounding the diagnosis of deafness. Paper presented at the Workshop on Needs of the Hearing Impaired. Crippled Children Services, Minnesota Department of Welfare, St. Paul.

Vernon, M. 1972. Mind over mouth: A rationale for total communication. Volta Rev. 74(9):529–540.

Vernon, M., and Koh, S. D. 1970. Early manual communication and deaf children's achievement. Am. Ann. Deaf 115:527–536.

Vernon, M., and Koh, S. D. 1971. Effects of oral preschool compared to early manual communication on education and communication in deaf children. Am. Ann. Deaf 116:569–574.

Vernon, M., and Makowsky, B. 1969. Deafness and minority group dynamics. Deaf Am. 21(11):3–6.

Weir, S., and Emanuel, R. 1976. Using LOGO to catalyze communication in an autistic child. D.A.I. Research Report No. 15 Department of Artificial Intelligence, University of Edinburgh, Edinburgh.

Wilbur, R. B. 1976. The linguistics of manual languages and manual systems. In L. L. Lloyd (ed.), Communication Assessment and Intervention Strategies. University Park Press, Baltimore.

Wilbur, R. B. 1977. An explanation of deaf children's difficulty with certain syntactic structures of English. Volta Rev. 79(2):85–92.

Wing, L. 1972. The handicaps of autistic children. In AUTISM — Proceedings of the 4th Annual Meeting of the National Society for Autistic Children, pp. 106–122. Flint, Mich.

Wing, L. 1976. The principles of remedial education for autistic children. In L. Wing (ed.), Early Childhood Autism. 2nd Ed. Pergamon Press, London.

Withrow, M. 1978. Computer animation and language instruction. Am. Ann. Deaf 123(6):723–725.

Woodward, J. C. 1973. Some observations on sociolinguistic variation and American Sign Language. Kansas J. Sociol. 9:191–200.

Yasaki, E. K. 1975. It's not your usual programming class. Datamation 21(12): 113–117, 120.

Index

Page numbers followed by *n* indicate footnote; *p* indicates picture.

Abnormal behaviors as adaptive and healthy, 32, 83, 89–91
Activity
  cognitive development without, 42–46
  for deaf child, novel sources for, computer as, 126–140
  dependence of cognitive development on, 39–48
  redefinition of, need for, 157
  varied meanings of, 43
  without interaction, effect of, on cognitive development, 46–48
Adaptive equipment, electronic, 6, 16
Adaptive value of symptom, 32, 83, 89–91
American Sign Language (ASL) for deaf, 23–24, 23*n,* 58–59, 65–66
  information transmission rate, 59
  size of lexicon, 66
Analysis of turtle drawing, 109–111
Anna, 152
Annette, 16, 80–81
Assessment, redefinition of, need for, 156–157
  problems in, 36, 58, 72, 156–157
Athetoid person, physical skills of, feedback for improving, 122–124
Attention in cognitive development, 42, 50
Autism
  abnormal response to sound, 83

characteristics of, 82–88
as misdiagnosis of deaf child, 56
prevalence in population, 7
symptoms of, as healthy, adaptive effort, 89–91
Autistic child(ren)
  characteristics of, 82–88
  communication abilities of, 85–87
  computer for communication needs of, 24
  difficulties of
    with nonverbal language, 84–85
    with social situations, 83
    with verbal language, 83–84
  experience of, with drawing with turtle, 72–76
  kinesthetic communication for, 86
  needing to initiate or control, 26*n,* 84–85, 140–145
  novel sources of meaning for, computer offering, 140–145
  perception and cognitive development in, 71–91
  perceptual problems, 82–84
  prosthetic device for, 24
  in school, 88–89
  unresponsiveness to gesture, 83
  see also JJ; Joey; Kevin; Nancy; Thomas
Autonomy
  dependency as expression of, 27
  dependency interfering with, 54
  developed from control and initiative, 26, 26*n*
  withholding effort as sign of, 27

Behavior
  normalization of, as goal of habil-
    itation of handicapped,
    30–32
  repetitive, in autistic child, 74,
    76–78
  as healthy, adaptive effort, 89–91
  need for re-examination, 156
Behavior modification, 89, 143–144
Biofeedback, 6
  movement, 122–125
  myoelectric, 124–125
  previous conceptions of, 119–120
  in speech training, 119, 121
  vocal, 120–122
Blindness and visual impairment, 6–8,
    31, 39, 152
  with deafness, 50, 87
Braille, 31
  usage by blind, 8
Brief experimental contact, 17,
    151–152
Bruce, 53p
Bruner on cognitive development,
    39–40, 42

CARIS program
  description of, 16–17
  experience of deaf child with, 56–58
Cerebral palsied child(ren)
  cognitive development in, 43–45
  computer, for, 27–28, 108–113
  demographic studies of, need for,
    157–158
  experience of, with drawing with
    turtle, 36–39, 109–113
  motor experience and cognitive
    development of, 35–51
  nonvocal, incidence, 14n
  prevalence figures, 13–14, 14n, 157
  see also Jane; Jay; Jonny; Ricky;
    Laurie; Susan
Cheryl, 113–115, 127
Child(ren)
  autistic, see Autistic child(ren)
  cerebral palsied, see Cerebral pal-
    sied child(ren)
  cognitively handicapped, 72–82
  see also Annette

deaf, see Deaf child(ren)
special, 33–91
  special technology for, research
    needs for, 149–166
Coded communicator, 105–107
Cognitive development
  of deaf children, 67–69
  dependence of, on motor activity,
    39–48
  research needs on, 153–154
  without activity, 42–46
Communicating with computer,
    96–115
  see also Computer(s), communicat-
    ing with
Communication
  aids for, technological lag in, 12
  handicaps involving, 23–25
  normal, components of, 23
Communication aid, electrical or elec-
    tronic, 5ff, 26ff
  coded selection type, see Coded
    communicator
  direct selection type, see Direct
    selection
  scanning type, see Scanning com-
    municator
Communication aids
  adaptation of, to child, 105–107
  for autistic child, 140–145
  experience of autistic child with,
    78–80
  experience of cerebral palsied child
    with, 36–37
Communication board, 31, 105–106
  not using a, 28
Computer(s)
  as animated scratchpad, 128–133
  as assistant, 21–22
  communicating with, 95–115
    input schemes for, 101–105
    space arrangements for, 101,
      103
    time arrangements for,
      103–105
    tailoring of, to child, 105–115
  composing on, 133–135
  control of
    eye-tracking for, 120
    headstick for, 120

limb movement tracking for,
122–124
myoelectric signals for, 124–125
vocal signals for, 120–122
educational uses of, 25–28
as entertainer, 21
as eyeglasses, 26–27
for handicapped, history of, 5–9
for interactive language games,
135–140
as mirror, 27–28
as source of activity for deaf child,
9, 118, 126–140
as source of control for physically
handicapped child, 119–126
as source of meaning for autistic
child, 9, 118–119, 140–145
as tutor, 25–26
Computer activities
cartooning, 22
color graphics, 22
music, 22
robot control, 22
speech generation, 22
Conferences, 7–8
Conservatism, intellectual, of deaf,
67–68
Cosmesis, 11, 120
Cost
of computer equipment for prosthetics, 22, 153
of support for physically handicapped, 14
of research, 150

Data tablet, 117p, 122–124, 123p
Deaf adults, 11n, 38, 61, 67
Deaf child(ren)
blind, 50, 87, 154
cognitive development in, 45–46,
67–69
communication needs of, 23–24, 30
education of
issues in, 60–61
oral/aural approach to, 63–64
total communication system for,
61–62
English, parsing by computer,
134–136

experience of
with CARIS program, 56–58
with drawing with turtle, 54–56,
159–166
functional retardation of, 86
history of computer work with, 9
intellectual conservatism of, 67–68
introduction of, to computers,
56–58
language and cognitive development
in, 53–69
language of, 65–67
novel sources of activity for, computer as, 126–140
prevalence, 6
special strengths of, 24
speech training aid for, 27
see also Bruce; Gary; Gordon; Jan;
Peter; Phillip
Deafness as educational handicap,
58–60
Demographic studies, need for,
157–158
Dependency as sign of autonomy, 27
Direct selection communication aid,
101–102
Disarthric speech, 121, 121n
Drill and practice, 9, 68, 89, 128
Dungeon as interactive language
game, 135n, 136–140

Editing, see Text editing
Education, deaf
issues in, 60–61
oral/aural approach to, 63–64
total communication approach to,
61–62
Educational handicap, of deafness,
58–60
Electric toothbrush, 11
Electronic mail, for deaf children,
131–135, 153
Employment possibilities, 9, 14, 15
Enactive representation and motor
learning, 39ff, 49
English, written
acquisition of, by deaf child
role of computer in, 127–140

English, written — *continued*
  as communication medium for
    autistic children, 86
  differences from spoken, 59–60
  difficulties of deaf with, 58–60
Enhanced feedback, for athetoid
  auditory, effect on speech, 124
  proprioceptive, effect on move-
    ment, 122–124
Exercise model of therapeutic inter-
    vention, 31
Experience, normalization of, 30–32
Eyeglasses as metaphor for technol-
    ogy, 4, 10*ff*, 31
Eye-tracking for controlling com-
    puter, 120

Fantasy play using computer, 74–75,
    114–115, 136*ff*
Feedback, 6, 20, 23, 25, 27*ff*, 134
  to establish meaning, 143
  need for, 29

Game, interactive English, computer
    based, 135–140
Gary, 90–91
Gordon, 17, 56–58
Growth, intellectual, theories of,
    39–48

Handicapped
  education of
    economics of, 13–15
    philosophy of, 9–12
    psychology of, 12–13
  needs of, 19–32
    normal, 20–21
    role of computer, 21–22
    special, 23–25
  physically, novel sources of control
    for, computer providing,
    119–126
  see also Autistic child(ren), Cere-
    bral palsied child(ren), Deaf
    child(ren)
Headstick for controlling computer,
    120

Hospital model of computer use, 26,
    126

Iconic representation, 39–40, 42, 49
Information
  need for in intellectual growth, 28
  transmission rate in communica-
    tion, 59
Intellectual conservatism of deaf,
    67–68
Intellectual growth, theories of, 39–48
Interaction
  action without, effect of, on cogni-
    tive development, 46–48
  in language acquisition, 68–69

JJ, 71*p*, 141*p*, 142*p*
Jan, 131–133
Jane, 11, 14*p*, 16, 27*ff*, 35*p*, 124–126,
    155
Jay, 16, 108–111, 115
Job skills and training, 9, 14–15
Joey, 16, 75–76
Jonny, 16, 112–113, 115
Joshua, 90
Juggling, 125–126

Kephart on cognitive development,
    40–42
Kevin, 15, 16
Kinesthetic communication for autis-
    tic child, 86

Language
  assessment, difficulties with,
    154–155
  of deaf child, 65–67
  development of, research needs on,
    154–155
  inner, of deaf children, 67
  learner, active involvement of,
    68–69, 127–128, 145
  nonverbal, difficulties of autistic
    children with, 84–85
  and thinking, relation between,
    64–65

verbal, difficulties of autistic children with, 83–84
Language games, interactive, computer, 135–140
Laurie, 112, 115
Learning, multimodal, in cognitive development, 49–50
Limb movement tracking for controlling computer, 122–124
Lipreading, see Speechreading
LOGO, 15n

Mail, electronic, for deaf, 131–135, 153
Meaning for autistic child, novel sources of
computer providing, 140–145
Mental retardation
definition, 81
functional, 25, 86
predicted by cognitive developmental theory, 43
presumed, 17, 27, 36, 109
prevalence, 7
relative, of autistic child in various tasks, 85
see also Annette
Mentally retarded child(ren), preverbal communication of, compared with autistic, 87
Metaphor for computer use
eyeglasses as, 4
mirror as, 27ff
tutor as, 25ff
Motivation of autistic child, 87–88
Motivational factors
in cognitive development, 49
in developing communication, 107–108
Motor learning, 39–51
Multimodal learning in cognitive development, 49–50
Myoelectric signals for controlling computer, 124–125

Nancy, 15–16, 72–75

Needs
normal, 20–21
computer for meeting, 21–22
and special, 19–32
special, 23–25
Nonverbal communication, 23
in infants, 87
Normal needs versus special needs, 4
Normalizing experience versus behavior, 30–32

Oral/aural approach for educating deaf, 63–64
Oral skills, 30–31
Organizations dealing with handicapped, 6

Perceptual learning, 40–41
Perceptual-motor development, requiring feedback, 30
Perseverative behavior
in autistic child, 76–78
as best available heuristic, 77–78, 90, 91
in emerging mental abilities, 89
as intellectual experiment, 74
in normal child, 90
need to redefine, 156
in preschool deaf child, 90–91
Peter, 16, 54–56, appendix
Phillip, 16, 56, appendix
Piaget on cognitive development, 41–45
Plotter, flatbed, as scanning communicator, 36–37, 37p
Pragmatics of language use
in classroom interaction, 59
in deaf children's language, 127–128
in developing language, deaf and hearing child compared, 58–59
influence on apparent expressive ability, 154–155
in physically handicapped children, 28–29
Prevalence figures
autism, 7, 86

Prevalence figures — *continued*
deafness, 6, 65
mental retardation, 7
physical handicaps, 13–14, 14n, 157
speech problems of cerebral palsied
people, 158

Reading instruction aided by computer
aid for blind, 8
level, prelingually deaf, 58
performance of autistic children,
76, 82
problems of deaf children, 54, 58
problems of normal children,
113–115
readiness, need to redefine, 156
use of computer without, 22
see also CARIS, 37–38
Repetitive behavior, *see* Perseveration
Retardation, *see* Mental retardation
Ricky, 16, 38–39

Scanning communicator, 31, 36–37,
37p, 96–107
flatbed plotter as, 36–37, 37p
Service delivery, research and development, needs for, 152–153
Sign language, 23–24, 23n, 30, 60, 60n
convention for transcription in this
book, appendix
used by non-humans, 151
Slot machine, 72–74, 73p
Social development, 155–156
Social situations, autistic children, 83
Spasticity
avoiding interference of, 124–125
using myoelectric control despite,
124–125
Special needs versus normal needs, 4
Speech
defect, 10
electronically produced, 22, 145,
152
electronically recognized, 22,
120–122, 145
skills, 30–31
training aid, 9, 27, 119, 121–122

Speechreading, 11n, 61–64
electronic aid to, 63
Spelling, inadequacy of communication board based on, for
physically handicapped, 106
Strengths, teaching toward, research
needs on, 157
Substitution model of therapeutic
intervention, 31
Susan, 16–17, 36–38, 108, 122–123
Symbolic representation and verbal
learning, 39–40, 42, 45,
49–50
Symptom as adaptive behavior, 32,
89–91

Teaching
computer as device for, 25–26
toward strengths, research needs
on, 157
Text editing, 8
computer, value for deaf children,
128–135
Theory versus value, 51, 64, 157
Thinking and language, 64–65
Thomas, 16, 78–80
Total communication for educating
deaf, 11n, 23n, 62, 68
Turtle, 13p, 149p
experiences of autistic child with,
72–76
experiences of cerebral palsied
child with, 36–39, 109–113
experiences of deaf child with,
54–56, appendix
how to draw with, 96–103
Tutor, computer as, 25–26

Value and theory components, dis-
tinction between, 51, 64, 157
Verbal learning, 42, 45
abstraction, 42, 51
Visual channel superior to auditory
in autistic children, 84
Visual fixation, in autistic children, 83
Visual memory in autistic, 84–85
Visually impaired, 7–8, 31

Vocabulary of young child, 64
Vocal channel for controlling com-
    puter, 120–122

Word processing systems, *see* Text
    editing
Written English, *see* English, written